WHY SOME CHRISTIANS COMMIT ADULTERY

Other Books by John and Paula Sandford

The Elijah Task
Restoring the Christian Family
The Transformation of the Inner Man
Healing the Wounded Spirit
Healing Victims of Sexual Abuse
Healing Women's Emotions
The Renewal of the Mind

John L. Sandford

Why Some Christians Commit Adultery

Victory House, Inc.
Tulsa, OK

Unless otherwise noted, all Scripture taken from the New American Standard Bible, © 1960, 1962, 1963, 1968, 1971, 1972, 1973, 1975, 1977 by The Lockman Foundation. Used by permission.

DEDICATION

To my wife, Paula:

For thirty-eight wonderful years as my
partner in Christ, lover and comforter,
mother of six, grandmother of thirteen,
and great-grandmother of one; and now,
in 1999, after forty-eight years of marriage,
still the mother of six, but grandmother of
twenty and great-grandmother of six.

And to Tony and Ami Lincoln

Our new son-in-law and our daughter,
for their work of editing and advice —
even while on their honeymoon!

CONTENTS

ACKNOWLEDGMENTS

This book would not have been written were it not for our publisher, Clift Richards of Victory House, Inc., and Lloyd Hildebrand, our long-time editor. They persuaded me that the book needed to be written, and that I should do it. The Holy Spirit confirmed and anointed — and I found it tumbling into my mind and onto the pages.

Special thanks to our at-home editor, our son-in-law Tony Lincoln, who spent many hours patiently turning my cumbersome thoughts into something readable. Many relatives and friends contributed welcome thoughts and advice, but of course none more so than my lovely wife. Our son Loren was inspired to preach a powerful sermon just at the right moment — which found its way into the book as the summation message.

My highest thanks to our Lord Jesus Christ and the Holy Spirit. I pray that the Lord will give to us all the wisdom to receive and apply His truths. The present epidemic of sin must come to a halt — quickly! It is to that end that I have bent every effort and burned a lot of midnight oil to write as fast as I could.

I pray that all will hear the call to repentance and intercession. Our Lord Jesus Christ will return for a purified Church prepared as a bride for her Groom. At present we remain a far cry from manifesting our Lord's righteousness. But take heart, "In faithfulness he will bring forth justice; *he will not falter or be discouraged* till he establishes justice on earth. In his law the islands will put their hope" (Isa. 42:3-4, NIV).

FOREWORD

In the first chapters I explain several not commonly known reasons why well-meaning Christians fall into adulterous relationships. But the greatest personal causes are the shatterings of personality and character in childhood. Fornicators and adulterers most often do what they do because of wounds and resultant fractures in their character that remain unhealed. They are impelled by unsatisfied hungers, by hidden needs to defile the opposite sex, to punish, to exact vengeance, or because others (including sometimes their own parents) molested them and/or involved them in some other form of lustful activity such as pornography.

Paula and I have attempted to help the Body deliver sinners from those traps through the teachings in Section Four of *The Transformation of the Inner Man:* Chapter Fifteen, "Fornication, Adultery, Inordinate Desire and Aberrations"; Chapter Sixteen, "Archetypes and Homosexuality"; and Chapter Seventeen, "Parental Inversion and Substitute Mates"; and through Paula's book, *Healing Victims of Sexual Abuse.*

In the first chapters of this book, we intend to reveal personal factors which induce normally wholesome, moral Christians to fall into sexual sins. None of us has received perfect parenting, and each has reacted negatively even to the best-intended parenting. All of us thus contain hidden areas of weakness (to say nothing of the vestiges of Adamic sin which continue to beset all of us after our conversion). But most of us aren't so deeply fragmented as to be *driven by compulsions.* We manage to subject our impulses to the correction of God's Word, and we are successfully constrained by not wishing to dishonor our Lord Jesus Christ. We seem to "have it all together" and may even congratulate ourselves that we *can't* be tempted by sexual sins.

Therefore, this book is written to help normally well-behaved, seemingly whole Christians who nevertheless can fall prey to conditions and pressures which can build until what have been controllable urges become compulsive and unmanageable habits. Since our will is always involved, none of us is entirely excused. We are not merely victims of what our society influences us to do. Therefore the book contains much tough love, and some warnings of severe discipline. But our main purpose is to provide *informed bases for compassion and healing,* and *keys of knowledge for protection from falling.*

This book is *not* written for those who set out purposefully to sin. God has but one admonition for such "Christians": *"Stop your sinning! Live righteously!"*

It is written in compassion and understanding, to impart forgiveness and healing to those who mean to stand but find themselves captured by forces they don't understand and can't withstand. It is written as well for all those who have been hurt and disillusioned by their actions. We write to equip the Body of Christ to aid the fallen and their victims, so that the Body may not blunder either by condemnation or misguided zeal. May God prosper the ministry of each brother and sister to one another as our Lord Jesus Christ sets out to heal His broken Body in these perilous times.

Section 1
Personal Causes and Cures
for Sexual Sins

1

Spiritual Adultery, Affairs and Physical Adultery

Christians seldom set out purposefully to commit adultery. Many find themselves wounded and perplexed that it could lay hold of them. Leaders especially, such as evangelists, pastors and teachers, are stunned to find that sexual sins they thought they would never fall into could so quickly bring them down! The Body of Christ reels in disillusionment, striving to comprehend how so many mighty men of God could be overcome. Christians and non-believers alike question how so many men who are responsible for the reputation of Christ before millions could risk so much for so little!

Powerful sexual forces can lay hold of men and women, whether or not they know the Lord. What confounds Christians is that sometimes they don't seem to be any more protected from sexual sins than non-believers! We shouldn't be surprised. We are subject to the same carnal urges, plus the fact that Satan doesn't work so hard to get non-believers into trouble. Why should he? Unbelievers are already in his kingdom. It is Christians he wants to destroy.

And many of us unwittingly help him do it! For the most part, Christians remain woefully naive about themselves as sexual beings, unaware of the forces in human nature which can bring them down, and consequently ignorant of the ways the powers of darkness can manipulate situations and sexual drives to plunge them into trouble. Truly, God's "people are destroyed for lack of knowledge" (Hos. 4:6).

SPIRITUAL ADULTERY

By the grace of God I have never sexually known any woman other than Paula. But that did not keep me out of *spiritual* adultery. My mother had seemed to me to be a very critical, wounding sort of person to be around. I therefore built walls; primary women were not safe to be near. That meant that early in our marriage, I could not freely share my heart with Paula — and this left me vulnerable.

God built us with a need to share. He said that it is not good for man to be alone (Gen. 2:18) and created woman to refresh man's heart. In my case, however, I was afraid to let Paula into my heart. Nature abhors a vacuum, so I found myself sharing things with others, both men and women in the congregation where I pastored, which ought to have been shared first and in some cases only with Paula — revelations, insights, hurts, fears, anxieties and hopes, whatever touched my heart and needed comfort or confirmation. It is Paula's task, and no one else's, to hold my heart in her care. But I had learned that whatever my mother knew ". . .can and will be used against you in a court of law!" Since Paula had replaced my mother as the primary woman of my life, I projected onto her that she would treat me as my mother did. I then reacted as though she had, no matter what she actually did. No way was I about to share more with Paula than I thought I had to.

Because of these experiences and feelings, I found "safer" places. It was expecially easy for me to open up to older women. Both of my grandmothers had been dear to me and easy to talk to. Therefore, older women posed no threat. They were not primary to me like Paula; so I could share freely with them.

Paula would overhear me at church gatherings talking about intimate things she hadn't yet heard, and it would hurt her terribly. She told me about it in no uncertain terms! I began to see that she was right, that I ought to have shared with her first. But I had no idea about spiritual adultery at the time, and I never had the slightest temptation to think *sexually* about any of the women I opened up to. I was young and immature and totally naive about what they might be thinking or feeling towards me. After Paula shared her feelings with me, I tried to remember to talk things out first with her, and thought that would take care of the problem. This meant that after making sure I had shared with Paula, I went right on opening my heart to other women, even if only in talking and sharing, in ways that should have been reserved for her alone. I couldn't see that I offered little real vulnerability at home and was only play-acting vulnerability "out there" where it seemed safer.

Paula, who is very spiritually sensitive, soon said to me, "John, I feel as though we aren't even alone in bed anymore! I can sense these women's spirits present with us right here in our bed!" There was nothing weird or occult about that. Wives often "know" when their husbands are involved in adulterous or potentially dangerous relationships. It's part of women's sixth sense to be able to feel it when another woman gets too close to their husband. Paula's words got my attention! Together we prayed for the Lord to reveal whatever might be causing it. We said, "Lord, if there is anything in John that still needs a mother, and somehow these women are being invited to fulill that need, heal that. Put the cross between John and any woman who might be drawn to try to fill any hurting emptiness in his heart."

We did what we call our "scatter-gun prayer." We prayed about every kind of possibility we could think of, just in case it might apply to me: "Holy Spirit, reveal in John anything which needs to feed his ego by turning women on to him — or just deal with it, whether he can see it or not." "If there is anything in John which unconsciously wants to punish women by turning them on and then turning them off by his high morality, bring that to death on your cross." "Jesus, if there is anything in John which wants to tease and play with sex outside the bonds of marriage, slay it." "Father God, whatever in John seeks any kind of fulfillment from women that You

designed to be fulfilled only by Paula, make John aware
of it — and slay it whether he sees it or not." "Lord, if
there are hidden, unholy sex drives in John, deal with
them now, before something catches him." Everything we
could think of, we prayed about, together.

Then we went after the roots of hurt in my
relationship with my mother and sister and every other
woman we could think of. Since I had been parentally
inverted (my father had become an alcoholic when I was
about ten, so I had become the strong one for my mother
and my younger brother and sister), we dealt with the
effects of that.

Parentally inverted people learn that the home is a
place of tension, not refreshment. They set themselves
always to be on guard in the home, lest chaos break out
and someone get hurt. So I had learned to find comfort
away from the house, out in the garden with my plants or
in the yard with my beautiful collie or in the barn with
my gentle and loving cow. These friends never hurt me
or let me down. They could always be counted on to meet
me with love and affection. It was therefore an ingrained
pattern in me to seek comfort outside the home with
others. That had to die.

After a few months of insistent prayer and searching,
we not only got those sinful patterns stopped, we became
aware of spiritual adultery. We understood then that a man
or a woman may be "dead certain" that he or she is true
to the spouse sexually, and equally sure that he or she
always will be — and be dead wrong!

I was probably not unique among young married
men. Most of us are quite naive about the types of
relationships we are involved in, and almost totally
unaware of spiritual adultery. Consequently, people may
already be deeply involved in it and be totally blind to it.

Paula used to say to me, "John, why didn't you tell
me you were worried about that? That's *my* job. It hurts
me when you tell somebody else first." Or, "John,-----didn't
need to know about that grief on your heart. That's *our*
business. I know you shared it with me first, but I wish

you wouldn't tell anyone else. Some day you'll know I'm the best friend you have." Or even concerning success and awards, "John, I don't want to be the last to hear about what's happening to you. It's embarrassing when people know more about what's happening to you than I do."

I was a late bloomer. Many, perhaps most, come to their marriages already having that sensitivity. But spiritual adultery is more subtle than my immaturity. Many women, married to men who seem to have little interest in spiritual matters, find a prayer partner with whom they can share their hearts — and may not realize they may be committing spiritual adultery with another woman. Men can commit spiritual adultery with co-workers, male or female. Unmarried people can develop habits of heartfelt sharing with friends — which may not die easily when a spouse comes to occupy that place in the heart.

Sharing is not itself adulterous. In Christ, we all need to learn to share the concerns of our hearts, more openly and accurately the more we mature in Christ. *Spiritual adultery occurs whenever, in the course of sharing, we grant to another than our spouse that position of comfort and refreshment which belongs first and someimes only to him or her.* God, through His Holy Spirit, is our first and greatest Comforter. But whenever He decides to do that through a human vessel, it is our spouse who has the first and greatest right to our hearts. Unfortunately, most of us have never heard of spiritual adultery; we remain untutored and blind in this area.

Therefore, I believe that the first and greatest cause of *sexual* adultery, among well-meaning Christians, is *spirtual* adultery. As I indicated above, spiritual adultery can be defined as any time married persons share with someone else what ought to have been shared first or only with their own spouses. Since anyone, believer or unbeliever, can open the heart adulterously, we need to confine our definition to Christians by saying that spiritual adultery occurs whenever, in the course of walking together in Christ, believers unwittingly open their renewed personal spirits to one another, sharing in heart and spirit what ought first or only to have been shared with their own husbands or wives.

Spiritual adultery is a distinctly Christian trap. Emotional or heart adultery can happen to anyone. Emotional adultery, though sometimes unintentional, is often consciously used by adulterous people to seduce others into relationships. They use emotion-laden glances and looks, body language, touches and suggestive words, whatever will signal intent and gain consent.

But *spiritual adultery bears this distinctive mark, that it is always* (at first) *unintentional.* Its participants are not purposefully sending and receiving signals. Initially, they are unaware of what is happening. That is one of the main reasons why Christians fall into adultery. If spiritual adultery were overt, especially if it wore recognizably sexual clothing, well-intentioned Christians would quickly shake free of it. But it isn't. It slips up unseen until Christians are so involved with one another, often so unaware of growing physical allurement, they fall into sexual temptation before they know what's happening.

Whenever spiritual adultery is persisted in, it leads inevitably to full physical adultery! After thirty years of counseling thousands of couples, trying to pick up the pieces of marriages shattered by adulteries, Paula and I can confidently say that we cannot recall any case that did not begin with spiritual adultery! (Remembering of course that we are speaking only of those who fell into it, not those who intentionally sought it.)

History and Anatomy of a Typical Spiral from Spiritual Adultery Into an Affair and Full Physical Adultery

A pastor sets out from seminary full of idealism. He intends to be a saint for the Lord, determined that he will maintain his high moral standards throughout his ministry! He may look with horror and shock, perhaps even with some condemnation, upon those he has heard about who have fallen, positive that such a thing could never happen to him.

His gift makes room for him (Prov. 18:16). Soon he is in demand beyond what he can handle. He begins to give up his Sabbaths, thinking it's a small-enough sacrifice he can make for his Lord, usually unaware that he is already in sin against God's Sabbath ordinance — God hadn't asked that of him; his self-importance did that. Soon, increasing weariness begins to affect his perceptions and judgment.

Now he finds that he can't share everything with his wife. That may be partly from the occupational hazard every pastor faces. We are all afraid that if we begin to share discreetly about what went on in the counseling office or about some other situation in the church, we won't be able to stop and we'll end up sharing what ought to have been kept confidential. We live in fear that someone will ask our wives questions they ought *not* to know the answers to, and when they do, we'll be in deep trouble! So we tend to avoid sharing at all. Pastors' wives often ruefully joke about how they are usually the last to learn what is going on in the church. If that kind of occupational hazard combines with hidden things in the pastor's heart such as were in mine, communication breaks down between the pastor and his wife. Eventually, he fails to share with her in all the other areas that have little or nothing to do with the church. She has become an "occupational widow."

Demands increase. More and more time must be spent at the office or in service somewhere for the Lord. His anointing increases. Miracles may happen. Crowds follow, and grow.

The pastor (evangelist, teacher, prophet) has now become drastically vulnerable to temptation — and greatly unaware! He is at the height of his powers, serving mightily, perhaps beyond what he ever dreamed or hoped.

But his heart has been dying. He has become a husk. He runs solely on anointing, empty emotionally — and needing — oh, so deeply needing.

Along comes the inevitable secretary (deaconess, choir director, prayer group leader, whatever...). His job demands that he communicate, if only for details of scheduling and planning. But that little bit is more than has been happening at home. He begins to share more than job planning with the other woman — after all, they need to talk things out in order to work in unity. He desperately needs someone who can understand him. His wife seems not to. Actually because she does so fully understand, she has been nagging at him to slow down. That, however, has only convinced him that she doesn't truly comprehend or appreciate the importance of what he is doing. He feels as though she just doesn't appreciate the "holiness" of the call upon his life — she "... doesn't understand me." He has become needlessly lonely and deprived.

If his sexual relationship with his wife has not altogether atrophied, he feels as if he is just going through the motions of making love for physical release. Since he isn't communicating with her nor meeting her at heart level, she feels as though whatever sexual requests he makes merely *use* her. It has become increasingly difficult for her to open to him, to give herself fully into him. That slays him emotionally, increasingly as demands continue to drain his already exhausted emotional reserves.

Meanwhile the close association with his co-worker has begun to stir strange emotions in his heart. It begins to be almost undeniably refreshing and healing to spend time with this partner in Christ. He begins to invent reasons to consult with her. His emotions come to life again. He senses anew the pulses of romantic feelings which had long been dormant. At first he projects them upon his wife and becomes a better lover at home. His wife wonders at the change, her relief tinged with apprehension. Before long he can't help but identify romantic feelings towards his co-worker.

Most likely she has been undergoing the same kinds of metamorphoses in her relationships at home and towards him. Whether she is married or not, she finds her association with this mighty man of God tremendously fulfilling. She calms her own rising fears about where this relationship is headed. After all, she is merely standing by him as a dutiful servant ought to, giving him the strength to carry on which no one else seems to be doing, not even his wife.

The man of God may begin to suspect that something is not quite right. Normally, he has never heard of spiritual adultery and has no training or knowledge by which to recognize its danger signals. All he knows is that it feels good and refreshing to be with his friend. When he examines his motives, he discovers no desire (as yet) to do anything sexual. To friends or authorities who try to warn him — or his wife — he may protest that this is a purely platonic relationship, necessary to the furtherance of the Lord's work. He may even chastise those who warn, telling them that they just don't understand a true Christian relationship — and maybe they have dirty minds and ought to repent — "The very idea!" Usually, however, the Body of Christ, ignorant of spiritual adultery and its dangers, keeps silent and merely worries and prays ineffectively (because God won't do what is *our* job).

As time progresses, so does the relationship. Now he is fighting down distinctly romantic urges. He wants to do special little things for her, like putting a bouquet on her desk and then deriving a secret thrill from seeing her delight. He starts feeling like a teenager. It feels so good to be coming alive again that if warning signals do go off in his head, his heart is too thrilled to allow him to listen. He knows that something is not right. Unaware of spiritual adultery, he can't figure exactly what is going on. He knows he ought to feel bad about what he is doing, but he feels so good, he can't make himself feel guilty. Besides, he tells himself, he hasn't actually done anything other than enjoy a few idle fancies. Maybe Jesus' saying comes to mind, that ". . .everyone who looks on a woman to lust for her has committed adultery with her already in his heart" (Matt. 5:28). But he tells himself that this Scripture couldn't apply to *him* because he doesn't recognize any lustful feelings toward her. Quite the contrary, he feels protective of her virtue, like a big brother. He has now become totally deluded about his actual desires and gravely unaware of his soul's jeopardy.

Sooner or later, the couple is thrown together in a situation where an opportunity for physical expression presents itself. It usually happens at a convention or on a trip somewhere. He may merely escort her to her room. But when he tries to give her a perfunctory Christian hug, suppressed feelings rise with a wallop! Whatever circumstances may have provided the opportunity, the two are gripped by forces they seem to be powerless to resist. Paula and I have counseled some who did initially have sufficient fortitude to rein themselves to a stop before they did anything more than heavy petting. But what has begun in them works on them until the opportunity comes that can't be denied. Eventually they wind up in bed together.

As servants of the Lord, both know they ought to feel terribly guilty, and maybe guilt does assail them. But they find it awesomely confusing that they feel so good! They had expected their sin would leave them sick at heart and overwhelmed with remorse. Though they may feel some guilt, what surprises them is that they don't feel overwhelmed at all. They feel sweetly cherished, in love, fulfilled, and inexplicably healthy! Their love-making cannot contain the fulness of glory which God designed for the sex act. That glory comes from the Holy Spirit singing the symphony of life and love through each to the other, spirit to spirit, heart to heart, body to body. *The Holy Spirit will not sing in immoral places.* But the level of their communication has opened their hearts to each other in ways and areas long closed to their own mates. Consequently their union has held far more excitement and pleasure than they have been finding at home. That thoroughly confuses them.

The couple then begins a process of justifying what they have done. Of course they *know* what they have done is sin and cannot entirely be reasoned away. But their relationship tells them they must really be in love with each other. Perhaps, they reason, they never actually loved their own spouses. After all, they had been so young. Now they are older and know their own minds better. This must be real love. If only they had found each other first. Surely God must understand — and now their minds are flooded with Scriptures about His grace and forgiveness.

At this point, they might determine to avoid ever getting into sex again. They vow abstinence. But their bodies have learned how to please and excite each other. They can't help finding ways to get together again.

Most confusing to the man of God is that he discovers that not only has the anointing not left him, he has become a far more stimulating and powerful preacher! His own struggles with guilt and fear, with self-hate and moments of grace, have prepared his mind, through the suffering in his heart, to reach people where they really are. He can better understand their troubles and struggles for faith because he is there himself. This further confuses him. He may remember that the gifts are irrevocable (Rom. 11:29), but he can't explain why he seems to be closer to God than before. Actually, God is pouring out His grace in order to bring him to fulness of repentance (Rom. 5:20 & 2:4). He, however, begins to reason that maybe he is so much more effective and God is so much closer because at last he has the right woman at his side, the one whom God must have planned for him in the first place. He thinks his repentance has already been full enough, because he has agonized for hours before God in the long hours of the night, wrestling with his confusions and guilts.

He may begin to entertain thoughts of divorcing his wife and marrying this woman, all the while dreading the moment when they will surely be discovered. He ruminates day and night, trying to plan what to do when that happens. If his children are still young, his heart is convulsed with grief and guilt, aching because he knows his wife will take them from him. The pain of anticipation becomes so intense he actually begins to long for discovery, so he can get it over and done with — and perhaps begins to do things unconsciously calculated to get them discovered.

Thoughts begin to plague him that, after all, this whole relationship may be delusion and a trap. Is he really willing to sacrifice his family and perhaps his entire ministry for whatever this relationship seems to be supplying to him?

In reality, what he thinks he has found with this woman is what his heart all along has yearned for with his wife. He does not realize that should he divorce his wife and marry his mistress, she will then be in the same position his wife now occupies — blocked out by remembrances of his mother and by the same occupational hazards which helped to break his ability to communicate with his wife!

His supposed love for his mistress is actually a delusion. He does not *really* know her, no matter how much he thinks he understands her heart as he never has any other. What he thinks he knows is comprised of fancies and projections of the "ideal woman," a dream world which inhabits the heart of every man. Throughout our childhood, all of us have gathered images of the ideal man and woman. Movies, novels, stories, mythologies and the Bible have implanted scenes of heroes and heroines in our memory stream. These act subliminally, drawing us to seek to find our heart's fancy. Soon after marriage, we discover that our mate is not that ideal dream person we thought he or she was. So the search unconsciously resumes. Spiritual adultery derives most of its power from the delusion that in this person we have at last found the fulfilment of our heart's dream.

The truth is that no one could ever fulfil our fancy's vision. No human being can be that ideal. But so long as the vision lives within our breast, it works to seduce us into continual fruitless searching. What happens to men involved in spiritual adultery is that the delusion grabs them that this woman is the very embodiment of that dream. They then project their emotional world into the care of their mistress, until they think they can't live without her. The same happens in reverse for the woman, who thinks she has found in this mighty man of God the one ideal man for her.

When he is finally caught, or confesses, or is in some way discovered, he is at first incapable of full repentance. To be sure, the grief he feels for what he has done to his Lord is enormous. What he has done to his wife and children wracks him to the core. And the shattering of his church nearly breaks his heart in two. *But all that pain is not to be confused with repentance. Repentance is born of God's grace,* granting to a man the ability to grieve, not for his own loss or his having hurt others, but *for their sake.* We knew a young man who did a lot of grieving that he had hurt others, but he never saw it in terms of identifying with their hurt, for their welfare.

A person may come to true repentance concerning the Lord, for the grief he has caused Him, for His sake. But the adultery snared him because his heart had not been fully open to his wife and family, and there is no guarantee that all that pain has yet opened his heart to her and to his children to think of their needs any more than he did before!

Some men choose their new-found "love" and leave their wives. In such cases it is obvious that repentance was not full nor healing complete. But some choose to stay with their wives. Here it may be more difficult to discern full repentance and complete healing. Such a husband feels closer to his wife, especially since her Christian heart usually enables her to forgive and stand by him through all the ensuing struggles.

What they are now struggling through together is rebuilding grounds of communication. Sex may now be great, since the pain of loss, and the new ability to communicate, may have reopened long-closed doors. But how sadly and how often we have seen such couples deluded into believing that at last they have fully and forever learned to communicate, that they have rediscovered their love (at great cost), and they will now be okay forevermore. That may not be so at all. *True repentance must "bring forth fruit in keeping with repentance"* (Matt. 3:8). He may be unusually attentive and sensitive for a while, and that also may delude her into thinking that she has a new husband. But true repentance for her sake will drive him to get at what ever formed the roots of their dysfunctions in their relationship from the beginning.

He will bend every effort to ferret out, with her, whatever may yet keep him from giving himself fully and unreservedly to her — hurtful memories of life with his mother, habits of withdrawal, bitter expectations that the woman of his life will disappoint him, etc. He will not abandon their search together until for her sake he has learned how to give his wife the rightful place God intended for her as the guardian of his feelings and the refresher of his heart.

Unfortunately, what we see happening most often is that their closeness immediately after the "event" convinces them that he has learned his lesson, and that he has become a truly sharing husband. But it may be that few, or perhaps none, of the primary reasons for his inability to share have been faced and dealt with. Consequently, sooner or later he reverts to the same habits of withdrawal, becomes vulnerable again, and falls for some other woman or to some other way of sinning which seems to relieve the pressure of his continuing loneliness.

ANTIDOTES

Antidotes can prevent sin before it happens, and/or prevent its recurrence afterwards.

The best antidote is wisdom. "For wisdom is protection just as money is protection. But the advantage of knowledge is that wisdom preserves the lives of its possessors" (Eccles. 7:12). Being aware of spiritual adultery has been a great protection to me through the years.

One might ask, "If spiritual adultery is so prevalent and deceptive, how can I avoid it?" Or, "How can I be free to share where I ought to, in support groups in the church and other places, especially with my pastor, if that may turn out to be spiritual adultery?!" Such fear is well-warranted. Good fear is part of our protection, "... work out your salvation with *fear* and trembling..." (Phil. 2:12b), and "The fear of the Lord is the beginning of wisdom; A good understanding have all those who do His commandments; ..." (Ps. 111:10). We must learn to let fear keep us alert. It is through *practice* that we learn to distinguish good from evil (Heb. 5:14).

Fear should not dissuade us from opening up to one another in the church. If we *don't* open and share appropriately in the church, we are not likely to at home either, and that will only increase our vulnerability to temptation. *Christians must learn by venturing.* Of course we are going to fall into spiritual adultery many times as we learn what and when to share and *not* to share with one another. But we don't have to abide in spiritual adultery a moment longer than it takes to recognize it and repent. If we are aware of the possibility, then by practice we can learn. Through trial and error I learned, until it became an automatic sensory system within me. Warning bells go off inside if I begin to share something private that Paula and I haven't yet had a chance to talk out. Alarm sirens sound within me if I begin to feel close to someone in ways that belong only to Paula.

It is helpful to know some principles, and we'll list those in a moment, but trying to recall them in the midst of a developing relationship won't work. They must be *built in* by practice and by determination to keep one's heart pure before God and one's mate — *before* we become that deeply involved. However, rather than avoiding all encounters lest we slip and fall, we must learn to risk, in small groups alongside our mate, where we can warn and teach one another. I had to learn to listen to Paula again and again when she would point out, "Are you aware that that woman's feelings towards you are not what you think they are?" After a while, I began to discern it myself.

We need to learn the humility of really hearing, until

truth that others speak to us becomes our own practiced warning system. But we must recognize even then we are not safe. Sometimes, for one reason or another, our own alarm system won't operate, or we don't hear it if it does. No matter what skills we acquire, we will always need the perceptions and counsel of others.

Some churches contain no "small groups" in which members can learn how to risk becoming vulnerable. Or their small groups are only "playing games," not becoming real with one another. Nevertheless, my father used to say, "Where there's a will, there's a way." Family members, not singly but in groups, friends, co-workers, neighbors, anyone close enough to know us can discern when we're "playing games," and act to counterbalance and warn. No one needs to walk alone.

How to Avoid Spiritual Adultery

First, *don't get isolated.* The enemy of our souls wants us to hear and live out that poem we all grew up with:

> I am the master of my fate;
> I am the captain of my soul.
>   From "Invictus," by William Ernest Henley

We are *not* the captains of our own souls nor the masters of our own destinies. Our Lord Jesus is. Through St. Peter, He tells us ". . . you also, as living stones, are *being built up* as a spiritual house. . ." (1 Pet. 2:5); not building ourselves by ourselves, but *being built by others.* And from Proverbs:

> A wise man will hear and increase in learning,
> And a man of understanding will acquire wise counsel. (1:5)

> The way of a fool is right in his own eyes,
> But a wise man is he who listens to counsel. (12:15)

Through presumption comes nothing but strife,
But with those who receive counsel is wisdom.
(13:10)

Where there is no guidance, the people fall, But
in abundance of counselors there is victory.
(11:14)

God wants His people to learn to be corporate, a
people who openly share their lives with one another.
It may be that part of the reason so many are falling in
these times is that we have failed to understand and
practice corporateness where He wants us to learn it in
relative safety, in small support groups in the Church.
Consequently, we are unprepared to deal rightly with the
proximity and intimacy we experience as He moves us
closer to one another as He builds His Church. Above
all, *do not become isolated from your wife.*

An excellent wife, who can find?
For her worth is far above jewels.
The heart of her husband trusts in her,
And he will have no lack of gain.
She does him good and not evil
All the days of her life.   (Prov. 31:10-12)

Or from your husband.

Wives, be subject to your own husbands, as to
the Lord. (Eph. 5:22)

. . . and let the wife see to it that she respect her
husband. (5:33)

Whatever the price may be to keep communication
flowing — full, honest and intimate — pay it gladly. If
openness fails at home, back down from the heights of
ministry for a while. Get your act together at home before
you attempt to scale those heights again.

The Lord God is my strength,
And He has made my feet like hinds' feet,
And makes me walk on my high places. (Hab.
3:19)

The hind, or mountain deer, can go safely upon the
mountain heights because wherever its front hooves step,
the rear ones follow exactly. In some places, were its back
feet to track even an inch out of line, the deer would
plummet to its death. Just so, our inmost hearts must be
trained to follow exactly where our renewed minds lead,
else we fall to temptations and disasters. We must build
into ourselves such practiced safeguards that we can safely
go upon the heights of service in the Lord — and that
practice begins at home. Pray through those possibilities
in the heart that Paula and I worked through — *together
with your spouse.*

Second, *learn about spiritual adultery, and what the
symptoms are to watch for.*

We have already discussed the nature of spiritual
adultery; the following are the most common symptoms:

1) The tendency to share private, intimate matters
with friends (or a certain friend) *before* having talked it out
with the spouse.

2) Spending inordinate amounts of time with one
member of the opposite sex, i.e., catching yourself invent-
ing *unnecessary reasons* to work alongside that partner in
the Gospel.

3) Finding more delight in being with some other
person than with your spouse.

4) Beginning to think that some friend *understands you
better* than your spouse; therefore you want to talk with
that one, but can't communicate as well at home.

5) *Unwillingness to hear* the warnings of others. You
stubbornly maintain that this is a platonic relationship and
are wounded that others can't see that; they seem
unwilling or incapable of trusting you.

6) Beware of *feeling youthful or "high"* around one
particular person who is not your spouse.

7) *Romantic feelings.* At first you'll transfer them to your wife or husband and think yourself a better lover at home — you may even find yourself ascribing your new ability to love at home to the "beneficial effects" of your relationship at work.

8) *Aggressive defensiveness.* Actually, you are trying *not* to admit to yourself that you are into something wrong, and so you project that onto others and attack whenever someone tries to give you a timely warning.

9) Be most leery when *opportunities arise to be apart* from the scrutiny or interference of others. Realize that our deceptive hearts are fully capable of setting up circumstances that appear innocent. Forbid yourself any opportunities to be alone with "special" co-workers of the opposite sex, and learn to recognize the increasing frequency of such "coincidences" as evidence of the sinful heart's contriving.

10) Finally, *watch for divisiveness.* Your heart, once engaged in spiritual adultery, will find reasons to disqualify your wise friends' warnings — and to listen to the unsound advice of fools. You will begin to alienate yourself from your longtime friends and find new ones who may seem better to you but are actually "yes people" who will let you go down the drain.

> Better is *open rebuke* than hidden love. The kisses
> of an enemy may be profuse, but faithful are the
> *wounds* of a friend.
> (Prov. 27:5,6,NIV)

Third, *if you aren't part of an intimate, committed small group, find one and join it.* Listen to what your brothers and sisters in Christ tell you. Value their opinions above your own, especially when they see things about you that you are sure can't be right.

POSSIBLE CURES

I say "POSSIBLE" because healing doesn't always come. It is not always possible to heal. There may be a chance if the victims are humble-minded, not too self-deluded yet, or may be capable of recognizing the power of deep, hidden motivations. If the marital relationship was so wounding that the adulterer is consciously or unconsciously looking for an escape, only a very high determination not to disgrace the name of the Lord can hold His servant to the pain of death on the cross long enough for the married couple to accomplish full healing. Most often, unfortunately, by the time a man comes for ministry, he has become so deluded about the actual nature of the relationship he is involved in that *he cannot hear* what wisdom would say to him.

A pastor came to me for counseling. He had been unable to communicate with his wife. He served a large urban church. Pressures had gotten to him, and he had committed adultery with his secretary. It was not difficult to see the history of spiritual adultery which had seduced them. I explained that, and tried to lead him into receiving forgiveness for his sin.

But he refused to hear what I said next: "Pastor, you must release your secretary from her job, and you must never allow yourself to see her again. Your bodies have learned a track to run on, and you will never be safe around her again."

He cried out, "I can't do that!"

"Why? You must."

"This woman is in my guts. I can't *live* without her!"

"Pastor, you can't live *because* of her. Let her go!"

"*NO!*

I tried unsuccessfully for quite a while to explain to him how he had identified his emotional life with her and that that kind of life was what he had always wanted with his wife and could still have. As I remonstrated with him and argued and scolded, I silently bound, to no avail, the stronghold of delusion which gripped his mind. Finally, I warned him that it was very likely that he would lose his church and his ministry and ever after forfeit his destiny if he did not cut free. He would not hear. I now see him every once in a while, a pastor without a church, wandering about looking for a place to minister, serving as a less-than-successful marriage counselor here and there, a broken man — whose wife has forgiven him and now stands by the shell that remains of a once noble and powerful servant of the Lord!

The *first lesson of healing* is that those who have fallen into an adulterous relationship, whether or not it ever resulted in physical adultery, must *release one another totally in the Lord*. They must cut free from one another and disavow the relationship completely. *They must be willing never to see one another again.* If the couple work together or are part of the same family — the spouse of a brother or sister, for example — it may be impossible to obtain sufficient physical distance. That being the case, the adulterers must fiercely practice the discipline of emotional detachment — or they will not survive in the face of their continuing attraction to one another.

Here there is a great possibility of delusion. Sometimes the adulterers think they have "burned their fingers" so severely they could never again get near the fire — but they can, and if the causative factors are not fully dealt with, they most likely will. Their spouses may catch them looking with longing glances at one another at church or family gatherings, though they themselves may be unaware their looks carry such freight.

Subconsciously they will be watching for "innocent" opportunities to be together — and are apt to become huffy if someone says something about it. "What's the matter? Can't you people ever just forgive and forget? Give us a break. We weren't doing anything." Maybe they weren't. Perhaps they have a right to be offended in that moment. But if either or both are wise, they will realize the danger and avoid even the appearance of evil. Friends and relatives will be doing them a favor by watching them closely for a while: "And have mercy on some, who are doubting; save others, snatching them out of the fire; and on some have mercy with fear, hating even the garment polluted by the flesh" (Jude 22,23).

Being watched like that may seem oppressive or

unfair. The adulterers must be taught to receive it humbly, that it is for their good. It will be only temporary, until discernment among the church and/or family agrees that their hearts are indeed as clear as they think they are. Spiritual adultery, whether or not it included physical sex, must not be played with. There are no heroes in these affairs; there are only living cowards. Once a couple has walked in the sacred ground of each other's hearts, pathways are etched into them which lead immediately into improper closeness, and to physical hungers which cleverly and greedily seek ways to find expression.

The *second lesson of healing* is that there must be *prayers for separation of their personal spirits from one another.* God has so built us that the first woman a man enters, his spirit latches on to that woman to protect her, provide for her, and bless her with his own love for the remainder of his days. In like manner, a woman's spirit latches on to the first man who enters her, to nurture and fulfil him all her days, to bless him and bring forth children to him and only to him. For that reason Scripture says that he must marry her. If he does not, and marries another, she is undone. From then on, her spirit will be seeking to fulfil a man she can never marry. "And if a man seduces a virgin...and lies with her, he must pay a dowry for her to be his wife" (Exod. 22:16). (Some have held to these Scriptures so legalistically that they have tried to bind young people to obviously wrong marriages. Let's remember that our Lord can heal and set free, and He can find wiser answers than strict adherence to the letter of the Law.)

The point is that *our spirit never forgets that union — or any other union.* It still seeks each one with whom we have lain, however many that may have been, no matter how long ago, nor how completely the mind has forgotten them.

Paula and I were teaching on a college campus about the glory which God has reserved for the marriage bed. Young men and women approached us afterwards with tears streaming down their faces. They said, "We've already lost the glory." A number reported that there had been so many, they couldn't even remember the names of all they had slept with. We listened to confessions far into the night. Over each we prayed, "We pronounce in the name and by the blood of Jesus that you are forgiven and washed clean. *We take authority and declare that your spirit is loosed from every man (or woman) with whom you have slept.* We direct your spirit to forget each union. We set you free to be open and present only to your own mate when that time comes."

We knew their minds would not forget their sins, and should not for humility's sake. But their spirits would forget to latch on to their former lovers, and they would be free and whole again. The next day those young people came to us absolutely radiant! Lines of care had gone from their faces overnight. Shadows were gone from their eyes. Their faces shone anew with youthful vigor and freshness. They exclaimed, "We feel so whole again! We hadn't realized how *scattered* we felt!" Of course. Their spirits had been fairly exhausted, trying to find and nurture all those long-forgotten lovers!

> Do you not know that your bodies are members of Christ? Shall I then take away the members of Christ and make them members of a harlot? May it never be! Or do you not know that the one who joins himself to a harlot is *one body with her?* For He says, "THE TWO WILL BECOME ONE FLESH." But the one who joins himself to the Lord is one spirit with Him. *Flee immorality.* Every other sin that a man commits is outside the body, but the immoral man sins against his own body. Or do you not know that your body is a temple of the Holy Spirit who is in you, whom you have from God, and that you are not your own? For you have been bought with a price: therefore glorify God in your body.
> (1 Cor. 6:15-20)

Because the two do become one flesh, we who minister must be careful to separate them. We have authority in Christ to do that: "Truly I say to you, whatever you shall bind on earth shall be bound in heaven; and whatever you loose on earth shall be loosed in heaven" (Matt. 18:18). Without that, adulterers will be drawn subconsciously to each other, day and night, without relief, perhaps never knowing why. They may be unable to understand why, when they have renounced the relationship and want to cut free, they keep being pulled back, as though an invisible magnet were drawing their thoughts and feelings to one another again. That may reconvince them that they really did love that person and never should have let go. Many have fallen back into old adulterous relationships because of this simple fact of union. Truly God's people are "destroyed for lack of knowledge."

The *third lesson of healing* is that those who minister should see to it that the roots of dysfunctioning between the husband and wife are crucified, and true ways of being corporate and expressing that corporateness are released and trained into the couple. If counselors do not "strike while the iron is hot" to expose those roots from formative years and bring those to death, the couple will sooner or later lose their rediscovered ability to share. And unless the man and his wife are loved by the Lord (with Christ's love through the counselor and the Christian community) into the capacity to be truly corporate, the glory God wants to give their relationship will surely disappear.

How to bring to death what needs to die and bring to life the way of Christian corporateness is not the subject of this book. That would and did require two entire books. I refer the reader to two of our previous books: *The Transformation of the Inner Man* and *Healing the Wounded Spirit* (both published by Victory House, Inc.). Suffice it to say that laying the ax to the roots is an absolute prerequisite if the man and his wife are to reach the fulness of blessing which alone can prevent recurrence and keep him (or her) closed to temptation in the future.

A good workman will hold the couple to the task until complete healing and transformation have been accomplished by the Lord.

Finally, *there must be healing in relation to the entire family and to the local Body of Christ in which each of the participants is a member.* I leave it to the wisdom of the elders in each situation to decide how much needs to be openly discussed and where. There are too many variables in each instance to spell out specific actions to be taken. Sometimes things just need to be talked over in private, between the elders and the participants alone. In one case we know of, an elder of a church came and confessed his sin of adultery to the other elders. They fully and adequately administered healing and the necessary disciplinary steps. But then he felt he should confess his sin to the entire body in a Sunday morning service. The elders knew that kind of unnecessary confession could only shock and wound the new Christians in their midst. They forbade him to do it — and almost had to fight him to keep him quiet! Sometimes public confession *does* need to be made, for instance when gossip about the sin has already spread throughout the body. Such confession could bring healing. But each case must be weighed on its own merits. *The one principle we would suggest is that the decisions about which actions might be appropriate never be left to only one man or woman.* No one person contains that much wisdom, and so much weight should never be placed on the shoulders of one alone. Nor should one bear alone the disfavor of those who might react or rebel against the decisions. "Without consultation, plans are frustrated, But with many counselors they succeed" (Prov. 15:22).

RESTITUTION

One more aspect should be addressed: *restitution.* Almost no one today knows anything about this forgotten scriptural principle. Many think the need for restitution died when Jesus paid the price for our sins on the cross. But it is not merely an Old Testament practice no longer required in Christianity. *Restitution is a necessary act for the restoration of loving hearts in relationships.*

For instance, if my neighbor borrows my lawn mower and it breaks while he is using it, and then he brings it back *without repairing it* and asks me to forgive him, I will do so; but a part of the trust our relationship is built on has been broken. I will still be his friend, but I am not so likely to trust him with anything of mine again. A strain has now crept into our relationship. If he does repair my lawn mower, returns it and asks forgiveness, that's better. But my lawn mower is now of less value than it was before it was broken. Something is still missing. My heart feels it, and my spirit is checked a bit in relation to my friend. But if he fixes my lawn mower, asks forgiveness, and brings me the gift of a new hedge trimmer, to more than make up for the damage, my heart is wide open to my brother! He can borrow anything of mine anytime he wants to! He has demonstrated that he will go extra miles because he is concerned for me and wants to keep my trust and love.

Exodus 22:14 says, "And if a man borrows anything from his neighbor, and it is injured or dies while its owner is not with it, he shall make full restitution." Verse one in the same chapter lays out rules whereby a thief shall restore five oxen for one, or four sheep for one. Zaccheus, knowing that the law for fraud required only that he repay in full and add one-fifth (Lev. 6:1-5), proclaimed to our Lord Jesus that he would repay *fourfold* (Luke 19:8), the same amount required for restitution for a lost sheep! In effect, He was saying to the Lord, "I know that these who feel I have defrauded them are as beloved sheep to You. Therefore I am willing for Your sake to repay as though I have wounded Your sheep. I love and honor You that much." He *knew* that Jesus is indeed the Good Shepherd. Here we see an instance of restitution in the New Testament; not denied, but honored by Jesus who responded by saying, "Today salvation has come to this house..." (Luke 19:9).

Those who have fallen into adultery and are truly

repentant should be helped by their church authorities to determine some form of restitution deemed adequate by all concerned to restore trust within the church fellowship. Authorities might assign some menial tasks for a time, such as cleaning the restrooms or doing some of the janitoring; or require that the offender sit in with counselors (in like cases if possible) where counselees would allow that. Nothing makes us more aware of the heinousness of sins than having to sit as a counselor, trying to repair the damages! Another possibility would be to or insist that the adulterer serve a number of hours in one of the church's ministries, such as to prisoners in jail, or to drunks on skid row.

Some one, or group, needs to be assigned to see to it that the restitutionary acts are carried out, and to observe and report on the attitude in which they are being done, and what good may be resulting from the process.

A fallen and restored husband should set himself some series of small but tender actions in order to win over his wife's heart to trust him again. Obviously, the same can be said about a fallen wife. There is nothing wrong with talking it over with the spouse and deciding together what might best heal and restore. Whether or not restitution becomes a joint project, the spouse and all the family should be careful lest they fall into one of two opposite pitfalls. On the one hand, a spouse or the family may be tempted to want to exact vengeance, demanding that the sinner "pay to the last farthing." On the other, Christians are more commonly tempted to be too easy on one another. It is not enough merely to confess and ask forgiveness. A wise man or woman will seek counsel from the pastor and elders as to what they think might be sufficient to more than make up for the harm they have done. Restitution must be tough enough to write lessons on the sinner's heart and to reassure and build trust in the rest of the family.

If the sin is not publicly known, unobtrusive tasks can be assigned, the performance of which may convince the elders that here is a truly repentant and restored sinner made whole.

A Few Mop-up Questions

If spiritual adultery is so common and prevalent, how can any pastor or counselor serve the Lord without getting into it? The answer is that it is nearly impossible! I am *not* saying that any servant of the Lord should decide to let spiritual adultery into his life! But there's a vast difference between Christian and secular counseling. Secular counselors are trained to be detached. All of us are familiar with the stereotype of a patient reclining on a couch, his analyst or psychiatrist sitting behind him scribbling notes on a pad, his alarm clock poised to ring to an end the "fifty-minute hour" of listening — the picture of detachment. Christian counseling and ministry, on the other hand, is *involved*. Our loving Lord ministers through us as we meet others. We are at risk. The Lord puts His trust in our ability to become involved in righteous ways that heal.

But those who come for help may not be able to keep their hearts pure in relation to us. Many times I have sat and listened to a woman pour her heart out. I know that the understanding and compassion she is getting from me is what she has always wanted from her husband, who has seemingly been incapable of giving it to her. I know how that can seduce her in the realm of her feelings towards me. I can sense when she begins to slide into adoration of me. We can't keep that kind of false love from happening altogether. Counselees and parishioners *will* fall in love with us. It is our task to understand what those feelings actually are, not to become confused nor offended by them, and to hold the line in righteousness, discussing the feelings with the counselee when that becomes necessary and appropriate to his or her healing.

"Where no oxen are, the manger is clean, But much increase comes by the strength of the ox" (Prov. 14:4). Counseling is necessarily a messy business, more so even than a pastor's job. It need not become a trap into delusion, though. We have wept over those counselors who thought their pretty young counselees' indications of love meant that they had really fallen in love with them. Again, knowledge and wisdom protect, and a lack of knowledge destroys. *Let everyone who ministers beware of spiritual adultery, and learn how to handle it uprightly for the sake of those whose spiritual welfare depends on their wisdom and righteousness!*

What should a spouse do who sees the mate becoming involved in a spiritually adulterous relationship? Warn. If that isn't heard, warn again and again. *Fight for your marriage.* Of course you are not the primary cause of your mate's confusion, but it would be wise to ask yourself in what ways you may have left your loved one vulnerable. *Get at your own failings in the marriage.* If trouble persists, find a counselor, and seek first to deal with your own root causes of dysfunction. Do not pout and scold. Do not give your loved one ammunition to confirm that it was right not to share with you! Let your troubles drive you to the Lord to sweeten your nature and make of you the kind of mate who is an invitation to find rest and healing at home.

What can loved ones say to friends and neighbors who ask what is going on? As little as possible. If perceptive people say, "Come on. I know something is happening," and you know you can't avoid answering something about it, tell them just to pray for you right now, that you are working on what it is, you appreciate their concern, and they don't need to know any more than that. If the questioner is a proper authority in the church, share whatever you can at the moment, and then tell your spouse that that authority is asking questions, and suggest that the two of you talk things out with him. You may receive an angry protest, but at least you have opened the door to healing.

What should I do if the one I see heading into spiritual adultery (and maybe into an affair) happens to be my pastor? First, pray. War against the powers of darkness which are trying to push him beyond dalliance into the hell of adultery. Speak to him about it. Get him to promise to read something informative such as this chapter — or read small portions to him. If he won't listen, take a friend, at best an officer in the church, and talk again. Finally, go quietly to whoever holds authority in the church and let them know what you see and what you have done. (In following these steps, you will have obeyed the scriptural admonitions of Luke 17:3 and Matthew 18:15-17.) If the authorities are not sufficiently informed to see the danger, get informative materials into their hands. Then be still and pray fervently.

2

Defilement, Affairs and Adultery

Defilement in the Counseling Office

A woman came to me for counseling. She was not at all the type of person I would consider attractive. Even if I had not been determined to be moral in Christ and locked into fidelity to Paula, there was no way I would have been interested in her sexually! As we visited, however, I was surprised to find immoral thoughts flooding my mind: "I want to tear this woman's clothes off." "I want to take this woman to bed!" While trying to appear outwardly calm and interested in what she was saying, I frantically searched my mind for answers: "What's going on here? How come thoughts like these are invading my mind? I know I don't want to do anything sexual with this woman, so why am I thinking thoughts like these?!" An idea dawned on me, so I asked her, "Since you came in here, have you been thinking lustful thoughts toward me?" Fortunately, she was the kind of woman who could hear such a question and not be offended. She answered truthfully, "Yes, pastor, I have, and I'm sorry."

Through my empathetic, burden-bearing nature, her feelings had come into my heart. My mind translated them as my own! They were not mine at all, just hers; but they expressed in me as though they were mine alone. That is what I mean by empathetic defilement.

Who hasn't met someone for the first time and surprisingly felt revulsion, immediately wanting to get away from that person? We can't sense anything outwardly about that person which could warrant such strong feelings. Why such a reaction? Sometimes that individual triggers memories of someone in our past who hurt us. More often there was nothing in ourselves that caused the feelings; they came from within the other. One time a counselee I had never met before came for a session. I felt rising within myself a strong urge to smash him in the face! By then, I had learned to use such things as clues for counseling, so I asked him some questions. He had been beaten by his father as a child, and as a teenager had been violently attacked many times by youthful gangs. His bitter-root judgment and expectancy to be treated violently had come into me as though it were my own, and my mind had obligingly provided thoughts and visions of me bashing him! That is defilement. "See to it that no one comes short of the grace of God; that no root of bitterness springing up causes trouble, and by it many be *defiled*" (Heb. 12:15).

Empathetic defilement is the permeation of our personal spirit by what is in others' spirits, which can be dangerous and confusing among servants of the Lord because our mind sometimes translates what we encounter in others as though it were our own.

Empathetic defilement is common throughout society. Recently, after Paula and I had taught in a church, a pediatrician excitedly proclaimed his thanks for the teaching on empathetic defilement:

> At last I understand what has been happening to me in my office! Sometimes when I have been talking to mothers about their children, I have found myself feeling frustrated, angry, busy and bothered. But my schedule isn't that busy. I don't have any reason to be angry; and I love my practice. And sometimes I feel confused and afraid. But I am well-trained, and confident of my skills. It didn't make sense why I should feel that way. Now I understand! Those weren't my feelings at all! That's what those women were feeling about their frustrations and fears as mothers! I picked up on their feelings, and my mind made them seem as though they were my own. I can see it all so clearly now. It's so simple! I feel so relieved!

And then a choir director came and said that she too felt great relief:

> You've helped me understand something that has been bothering me for a long time. I *know* I'm a skilled musician. I've been trained to control my diaphragm and my breathing, and how to place sounds rightly so as to sing correctly. I've been a choir director for many years, so that it's built into me to keep the right rhythm and tempo. I'm a good director. But sometimes I'm plagued by the weirdest thoughts and feelings, like 'I don't know how to do this' or 'What's that symbol mean?' (when I know perfectly well what every note and symbol on the entire score calls for). And sometimes, for seemingly no reason at all, I feel so shaky and scared inside that I can hardly concentrate or keep time, and my ability to breathe leaves me, until I wind up as breathless as a rank beginner!

> "Now I see what's been happening. Most of my choir members aren't trained. They're just volunteers. Often they don't know how to read the score and they are afraid. I tune in to my choir so as to be one with them. I'm being defiled by what's in them!

> It's such a relief to know that!

She went on to explain that she could understand empathetic burden-bearing. She had often felt the burdens of others in her heart. But she had not known about empathetic defilement. What had confused her was that the thoughts and feelings of her choir members had arisen within her as though they were her own: "I don't know how to sing this." "What does that mean?" "I'm afraid." She exclaimed, "I don't have to let those things bother me anymore. I'm okay!"

There are two kinds of defilement: general and empathetic. Paula and I wrote about both in our book, *Healing the Wounded Spirit*. I quote here from Chapter Eight, "Defilements, Devils and Death Wishes."

Have we not all had occasions of being next to someone who radiated sexual uncleanness? Women tend to be more keenly aware of this than men. Many times wives have walked away from some chance meeting to fill their husband's ears with warnings about "that fellow," usually to the husband's bewilderment. "Hey, you just met that man! How can you know all that about him? Don't you think you're being a bit hasty and judgmental?" Later on he may discover that the fellow had seduced half the women in his office! She felt defiled in his presence. She knew. Wise husbands have learned to give some credence to such perceptions, at least to look for the outcropping of possible weeds in the garden. [The above is an example of general defilement.]

Haven't we all met some people who instantly caused us to feel on guard? I remember hearing my friend who was a pastor raving about a teacher who had come from another country and was teaching in his church. I was curious, and strangely worried in my spirit. My friend sensed that and arranged for us to have breakfast with him and his traveling companion. I liked the teacher. My spirit could trust him. But what an evil presence radiated from his companion! My spirit sang out inside me almost audibly, "Enemy! Enemy!" I felt unclean inside myself in his presence, unsettled and wary. I knew him to be a wolf in sheep's clothing.

I warned my pastor friend. But he could not hear me. The teacher returned home. His companion stayed, and ripped that congregation to shreds! According to him all art works and musical scores had to be thrown out of every home, unless they had the face of Jesus on them. They were of the devil. He pronounced curses over most of the congregation when they would not surrender to his wishes. Women in the congregation were told they would have uterine cancers if they disobeyed him, or if they merely disagreed. The congregation finally rose up and threw him out, along with my pastor friend, unfortunately. But worse yet, nearly a third of the congregation, the babies in Christ, were defiled by his spirit and left to join him in delusion.

In this story we see the operation of the gift of perception of spirits on the basis of our spirit's ability to feel what is in the other, to sense and identify defilement. We may possess that gift purely from God, but it grows by experience, "But solid food is for the mature, who because of practice have their senses trained to discern good and evil" (Heb. 5:14). The import of this story, however, is not to teach about the gift of discernment, but the danger to those whose spirits either are not keen enough or not sufficiently mature to beware. That man's spirit so infected and defiled the simple that they found themselves thinking in ways and saying things they would never have allowed otherwise. [The above is an example of empathetic defilement.]

Leave the presence of a fool, Or you will not discern words of knowledge. The wisdom of the prudent is to understand his way, But the folly of fools is deceit (Prov. 14: 7,8).

For a fool speaks nonsense, And his heart inclines toward wickedness, To practice ungodliness and to speak error against the Lord, To keep the hungry person unsatisfied And to withhold drink from the thirsty. As for a rogue, his weapons are evil; He devises wicked schemes To destroy the afflicted with slander, Even though the needy one speaks what is right (Isa. 32:6,7).

Incidentally, in about a year that man suddenly contracted intestinal cancer, and was dead in six weeks! One thinks of Herod, who was eaten by worms (Acts 12:23) and the magician whom the Holy Spirit blinded through Paul on the island of Salamis (Acts 13:1-12).

The tragedy in my friend's church was one of defilement. As I had found myself thinking strange thoughts in the presence of the people in our first examples, so these people found themselves thinking in that wolf's ways. We are not speaking of hypnotic spells nor of conscious thought-control techniques. That man himself was unaware of the demonic source of the influence of his spirit, though he had learned to depend on his ability to influence people. Later we will return to expound about the devils behind the scenes; for now, we focus purely on what emanates from our own personal spirits. The immature Christians in that church either lacked perception or experience or were simply overwhelmed. They were unaware of their defilement. They believed their thoughts were their own...
[This also is empathetic defilement.]

A word of caution should be added. The Hebrew people were very much aware of defilements, too much aware. Old Testament law mentions many things which defiled, and what to do about them — not at all repeated in the New Testament, which ought to tell us something! Many foods defiled (Lev. 11). Giving birth defiled (Lev. 12). Some diseases made people unclean (Lev.13). Accidental or purposeful ejaculation defiled, and so did women's menstrual periods (Lev. 15). Immorality, idols, touching dead bodies — hundreds of things defiled. Jesus found Pharisees performing four hundred ablutions a day just to wash away defilements. The word "kosher" comes from those days of careful washings and preparations designed to avoid defilement. Simon the Pharisee was convinced Jesus was no prophet or he would have prohibited that woman of ill repute from defiling Him by touching His feet (Luke 7:36-50).

Jesus countered this by letting His disciples eat with unwashed hands, and by teaching directly,

"Not what enters into the mouth defiles the man, but what proceeds out of the mouth, this defiles the man." Then the disciples came and said to Him, "Do You know that the Pharisees were offended when they heard this statement?" But He answered and said, "Every plant which My heavenly Father did not plant shall be rooted up. Let them alone; they are blind guides of the blind. And if a blind man guides a blind man, both will fall into a pit." And Peter answered and said to Him, "Explain the parable to us." And He said, "Are you still without understanding? Do you not understand that everything that goes into the mouth passes into the stomach, and is eliminated? But the things that proceed out of the mouth come from the heart, and those defile the man. For out of the heart come evil thoughts, murders, adulteries, fornications, thefts, false witness, slanders. These are the things which defile the man. . ."   (Matt. 15:11-20).

Once for all Jesus did away with exterior

fears of defilement and consequent rituals to cleanse. No Christian need fear defilement from outside by things.
[The above refers to general defilement.]

But He retained warnings of inner defilements; ". . . out of the heart come evil thoughts, murders, adulteries, fornications, thefts, false witness, slanders. These are the things which defile the man." Not what touches us from outside but what we feel inside and do outside, immorally or idolatrously, is what defiles.
[Taken from *Healing the Wounded Spirit*, pp. 204-206,208,209.]

While the Hebrew mentality of Old Testament days was nearly fanatical about avoiding defilement, in our day there is virtually no awareness of it, especially about empathetic defilement, among Christian leaders, pastors, teachers, evangelists, etc. Many of us expect to be protected by the Lord; we assume He takes care of defilement, so we don't have to worry about it. But in fact we have a job to do in this area, and the Lord is not going to let us off the hook. His warnings abound in the Scriptures. Here are just a few:

He who walks with wise men will be wise, But the companion of fools will suffer harm.
(Prov. 13:20)

Do not defile yourselves by any of these things; for by all these the nations which I am casting out before you have become defiled. For the land has become defiled, therefore I have visited its punishment upon it, so the land has spewed out its inhabitants. But as for you, you are to keep My statutes and My judgments, and shall not do any of these abominations, neither the native, nor the alien who sojourns among you (for the men of the land who have been before you have done all these abominations, and the land has become defiled); so that the land may not spew

you out, should you defile it, as it has spewed
out the nation which has been before you. For
whoever does any of these abominations, those
persons who do so shall be cut off from among
their people. Thus you are to keep My charge,
that you do not practice any of the abominable
customs which have been practiced before you,
so as to defile yourselves with them; I am the
Lord your God.

(Lev. 18:24-30)

Therefore, having these promises, beloved,
let us cleanse ourselves from all defilement of
flesh and spirit, perfecting holiness in the fear
of God.

(2 Cor. 7:1)

Repeatedly, our Lord warns and commands us to take
our own responsibility. In the Old and New Testaments,
the Lord speaks about defilement 116 times!

Defilement happens in two ways: by our sinful
actions, and by association with others. *It is defilement by
association we are concerned about in this chapter.*

A pastor I knew was counseling a parishioner, a
lovely young woman, whose father had neglected her
throughout her childhood. Within her was a tremendous
need to be comforted and held by a father. Neither she
nor the pastor were aware of the longings which fairly
beamed from her heart, drawing him to hold, or at least
to touch her. As they talked about the intimate problems
of her marital relationship, his sympathetic attention and
understanding opened her heart to love and appreciate
him. Gratitude welled up and merged with the ache in
her heart for her daddy to have done what this man was
now doing — receiving her. He was taking time from his
busy schedule, something her father had never done. She
could actually sense his compassion embracing her! It felt
so good!

Her crescendoing feelings entered his heart. His mind
took them as his own. Experience told him she was very
likely to have feelings of love towards her counselor. He

could handle that intellectually. What he was not prepared to understand rightly were his *own* thoughts and feelings towards her. That shocked him. Did he really love this girl? While she talked on, he examined his feelings. They were definitely not the usual expressions of *agape* love every pastor or counselor feels as he ministers. Scanning his memories, he found that she didn't remind him of any woman who had loved him in his childhood. He couldn't understand the attraction. He had counseled pretty girls before, but that was not what attracted him. He felt as though he wanted to possess her. His mind said, "I love this girl as my own." He decided, "She must be as a daughter to me." Actually, his mind had misinterpreted *her* desire for a father, resonating in his heart, as his own desire to have her as his daughter.

As they continued to discuss her problems, his intuitive and sensitive grasp of everything she was sharing so thrilled her heart, she began to wish she had married a man like him, one who could meet her spirit and refresh her heart. Her feelings had now become those of a wife hungry for her husband to know and embrace her at that deep level their courtship had seemed to promise.

The message now beaming from her heart to her pastor was, "Love me like a husband." She was not trying to seduce him. Had there been overt seductiveness, the pastor, who was a truly righteous man, would have sensed it and immediately confronted her. But he had no idea that something from within her could influence his own thought-world. The unusually strong empathy between them naturally made it easy for him to read her emotions and thoughts. In that sense, he was aware that her presence very much affected him. And it had been easy to detect any untoward emotions he felt about her, and to give those to the Lord and find freedom. What bothered him was that thoughts kept coming into his head telling him he was beginning to love this woman like a wife! When he put that together with the earlier feelings and thoughts of possessiveness, he found himself in a cold sweat. This woman was definitely getting to him! How?!

The mystery is solved when we know how defilement works. The pastor didn't really want to marry his counselee, nor she him. But her needs for her own husband to take her into his heart and shelter her emotions had spoken to the pastor's empathetic nature. His mind had interpreted those needs as though they were his own feelings and thoughts about her. Defilement was robbing him of objectivity in the counseling sessions.

The most confusing thing about empathetic defilement is that it does not always happen with every counselee. If it did, we could count on its happening and recognize it easily. But empathy is not always defiled.· Counselees' feelings and thoughts do not always arise within our minds in every counseling session as though they were our own. We sense and feel what is in the other and properly identify it as his (or hers). There is no defilement in it. Empathy has enabled us to feel what is in the other, and the Holy Spirit has helped us name the feelings accurately. Empathy is thus a great tool for ministry. By it we know what is in our counselees' hearts, and can direct our questions quickly to what is actually troubling. Empathy is one of the best channels by which the gifts of knowledge and perception operate within us.

Who can say why sometimes it becomes defiling and translates in our mind as our own? After thirty years of counseling, I still cannot determine why empathy becomes empathetic defilement with only a few of my counselees on rare occasions, though I have learned to recognize it and not be fooled by it. *My suspicion is that Satan, desiring to seduce us, waits until he thinks just the right person has come, and then steps in to block out common sense and judgment just long enough so we won't detect that we are running in the flesh. Then he can turn empathy into defilement and cause our minds to read what we sense as our own.* I had counseled for many years before that woman came whose lust translated as my own. I had never experienced that kind of thing until that moment. Perhaps Satan had miscalulated. Unaware of my aversion for her type, maybe he thought he could tempt me into sex with her, and tipped his hand so that I became aware of his game.

Some have simply lusted for their counselee(s), without the additional complication of empathetic defilement. And some may wonder how they can tell which is which. I'll address that later. For now, what makes it most deceptive is that empathy does not always become defilement. This pastor in our story had never experienced such feelings and thoughts arising within himself towards any other counselee. Empathetic defilement had never happened to him before, and he had no knowledge of it.

Recognizing his vulnerability, he referred her to another counselor. He tried to protect her from possible feelings of rejection by saying that she needed to talk with someone who might have more expertise. She saw through the excuse and left, hurting because "Daddy" had rejected her again! Sad to say, he needn't have cut short this ministry. It was actually making progress toward healing her deeply wounded heart. But without knowledge about defilement, an intolerable burden of restraint would have grown upon him as their relationship developed to the depths required for her healing. Those wounded by rejection from one parent or both need much more than being enabled to forgive. They can become whole only if they perceive that someone in the present does truly (and safely) love them, not sexually as a mate, but as a father or mother would care for them, to make them whole. Since the pastor did not understand his feelings and thus could not manage them rightly, he was wise to end the counseling relationship.

Knowing about defilement would have erased fear from his heart. He would have sensed during the session that his thoughts and feelings were most likely not his own, and then in the cool detachment of meditation afterwards he could have isolated them clearly for what they were: mere empathetic identification. Wisdom would then have enabled him to invite his wife or a co-worker to sit in with him as the relationship deepened into the kind of Christian love which could have thoroughly healed her heart.

Unfortunately, many servants are not so righteous or wise. Paula and I have counseled hundreds of people who have told us horror stories about "Christian counselors" who fell to making sexual advances while ministering to them! Many of these were simply lustful people who had no business counseling. Some intended to use their position as counselors to seduce people weakened by their troubles. "Christians" such as these use empathetic defilement to help them seduce their victims (though they may have little conscious awareness of what it is, having merely learned to rely on their power to overcome others). However, we need to remember that this book is not written for the purposefully sinful, but for those with good intentions who can be overcome by their own or, in this case, others' lusts. These servants, ignorant of defilement, and perhaps at the moment unwilling or unable to hold to God's moral standards, had believed the amorous feelings and thoughts in the counseling sessions had been their own. Delusion! None of their love feelings had been real. Real love in the Holy Spirit would have manifested our Lord's chaste compassion, and would have respected the holiness of the personhood of the other.

Countless Christian ministries have been brought down by affairs and eventual adulteries which began as nothing more than defilement!

When defilement joins with spiritual adultery, among those lacking the righteousness and wisdom of the pastor mentioned earlier, the result is almost always an affair. Defilement and spiritual adultery acting in tandem usually hook into unresolved issues in the heart of either the counselee or the counselor, or both. Unmet needs then cry for fulfillment. The resulting dynamics of the relationship become more confused daily, and devastatingly compelling. If those factors meet with dysfunction in the marital relationship of one or both, compulsive behaviors enter the scene. The people involved *must* see one another. They begin to concoct reasons for meeting outside the counseling office. At first it seems quite innocent, both to them and to others. After a while they can no longer resist natural urges, and they fall to physical adultery. Their history is then no different from what we described in the first chapter. The one difference is that, because they have believed the illusory feelings and thoughts engendered by defilement, they may be more adamantly sure that they are "really in love." They may, therefore, be less likely to come to true repentance and less apt to return to their mates.

SPIRITUAL DEFILEMENTS

A woman came to us, complaining of feeling defiled every time her husband made love to her. While we were looking into her history to find what could have caused such feelings, and were teaching her positively about the holiness of marital sex, she discovered that though they had six children and made love regularly, he had all along been a "closet queen" (an undeclared homosexual)! He had taken young boys to their cabin by the lake throughout their marriage, and had engaged in all sorts of gross sexual behaviors. No wonder she had felt defiled in the marriage bed! He was an unclean vessel. Being one with him meant that every time he was involved in gross sexual activity, she had sensed it in her own being. She had felt defiled even when apart from him, but most sickeningly when his uncleanness was joined to her in marital sex.

I call this a spiritual defilement because only in her spirit could she have felt, across space, what he was doing. There is nothing mystical or psychic about this. "And if one member suffers, all the members suffer with it; if one member is honored, all the members rejoice with it" (1 Cor. 12:26). Our corporateness means that we are so knit to each other that what happens to one affects all. When Achan stole the devoted things (Josh. 7), no one was aware of it. But that sin so worked on the consciousness of the people that the next day in battle their confidence was shattered and they fled in defeat. When Zimri and Cozbi entered into adultery, Israel was afflicted *immediately* by a plague which killed 24,000 (Num. 25)! *What we are and do either blesses others or defiles them!*

Defilement and blessing happen — whether or not we believe they can happen, want them, reject them or choose them. Blessing and defilement are the facts of our existence. C. S. Lewis said, "What we do or don't do has eternal consequences." We can't change those facts; but they will change us.

The import of this is twofold: On the one hand, every person is unique as to how he affects us by the blessing and/or defilement coming through him (or her). I remember counseling one terribly overweight lady who carried the extra burden of being quite ugly. Nevertheless, an extremely powerful seductive defilement radiated from her, and she confessed one sexual encounter after another! No man in his right mind could have wanted to go to bed with her! Her power had to be the force of defilement. Even if we were to ascribe her power to demonic influence, any demons would have had to work through the channel of human defilement.

A servant of the Lord can be safe from most people's defilements by being in himself a righteous person and by knowing about and guarding against defilement. And yet an individual can come to him so filled with spiritually defiling power that it may be all he can do to keep from being overcome by it. Several times when I have sat down to counsel someone, alarm bells have gone off in my spirit. Even with the warning, it took all my knowledge and experience, and the grace of the Lord, to minister to that person without being drawn by strange thoughts and feelings into wrong insights and decisions.

Any servant of the Lord who has ministered very long will recognize that demonic presences are quite often involved in that kind of warfare. Novices and the unwary can be swept away by spiritual defilement into adulterous feelings and thoughts, even into affairs and adulteries. Our suggestion: let beginners work with more mature laborers in the kingdom. Or, if that is not possible, let them make sure there are friends and loved ones (to whom they are subject) who can regularly check on them. Beginners should set themselves to heed the warnings of wiser, more experienced Christians.

Satan comes disguised as "an angel of light" (2 Cor. 11:14). People who outwardly seem wholesome can have within them foul torrents of defilement. Once we have begun to minister to them, our desire for them to become whole may blind us to what is actually hooking into us through defilement. Therefore, we give the same advice to long-practiced servants as to novices — listen to warnings. Stay close to trusted friends. Give them access to what's going on in your heart. When they warn that you are not safe, break it off, or bring a partner in to minister with you. Our Lord sent His servants two-by-two for good reason!

A lady friend of ours began to minister to a lesbian, hoping to succeed where many had failed. This woman had gone from person to person, from healer to healer, one counselor after another, ostensibly (even to herself) seeking release to normal sexuality. Nothing had helped. Eventually she learned to receive so much love by having problems that unconsciously she had no desire to become whole. Meanwhile, she had developed about herself an extremely powerful "field" of defilement.

Our friend soon found stirrings in her heart. She found the impulses to touch and hold this wounded creature almost impossible to refuse. But she rationalized, "Why not?" She was older than the lesbian, and her desires to touch seemed no different from the hugs she would normally have wanted to give to any other hurting woman. Unaware that the lesbian's desire to be touched and held was being transformed in her mind as her own desires, she ascribed their unusual strength to the greater depth of this person's need and the consequently stronger love she must have been feeling. She had never had any lesbian feelings, and thought of herself as a mature and practiced Christian who could surely recognize obvious lesbian approaches and not respond in kind. Therefore, the strong desires to hold and comfort neither warned nor frightened her. She was used to such feelings.

But she knew nothing of the seductive nature and power of spiritual defilement. The longer she ministered to the other woman, the more her heart went out to her. She ached for her to become whole and happy. Meanwhile the closer their relationship became, the more the lesbian desired to have sex with her. Our friend had no idea that another's feelings could be interpreted by her mind as her own. She was therefore disarmed when she began to recognize in herself distinctly sexual feelings toward her counselee. Feelings from the counselee towards her she had expected and was prepared to handle. But she had not expected the reverse. She thought those sexual feelings were her own. When they became stronger and stronger, she began to think that perhaps she had always had them, and this woman had merely come along and awakened them!

Sex with her husband had been waning, due mostly to her fatigue and a consequent breakdown in their ability to communicate. She began to connect that deterioration with the growth of these new desires, and thought, "Naturally. As I have begun to discover who I really am, desires for sex with him would begin to drop off."

At last, she tried sex with her friend and found it quite pleasurable! By now, defilement and the power of the stronghold of sodomy had so gripped her mind that she hadn't the freedom to notice that it had been distinctly unfulfilling, only merely surprisingly pleasurable. The stronghold kept her from observing the hollowness and emptiness her spirit felt. Under the impact of defilement, she could no longer remember the satisfying sense of completion and holy union she had felt so many times with her husband. The pleasure of feminine touch, aided by the stronghold of sodomy and its delusions, convinced her that she had at last found what was right for her!

Her Christian training nagged at her that she was committing adultery, but the powers of darkness now fed her mind with all the usual delusive thoughts and feelings. "How could anything that feels so good be wrong?" And, "If it's good *to* you, it must be good *for* you." Satan then withdrew his attacks upon her physical health (she had been suffering some nagging physical conditions which didn't seem to want to respond to medical treatments). Satan wanted her to feel vibrant and healthy, in order to add more confusions to her already-defiled mind: "How could I be healthier than I have been in a long time if I were really into something wrong? My health has gotten so good, it must be a sign that what I'm doing is okay!" Satan next withdrew all spirits of oppression and warfare. She felt light and free. "I couldn't feel this way if this relationship were wrong."

Satan can use both edges of the sword of defilement. First, he can seduce us as he was seducing our friend through her counselee. And second, when the hook is set, he can reel us in by removing the oppression of his defilement which every Christian battles daily. Thus our good feelings convince us we must be on the right track! Years ago I fell for a time into a delusion. The moment my mind agreed to that false idea, Satan immediately withdrew his attacks upon me. I concluded that the release I felt was because the "revelation" I had found was right! The same was now happening to our friend.

Friends tried to warn her, to no avail. She could not hear. They had become, "Cold and insensitive, lacking the care they should have had as Christians!" Well, she would show them. She, at least, would not give up on this girl as everyone else seemed to have done. Several months later, she did finally hear the warnings about lesbianism, repented of her error and received forgiveness. But she continued to try to minister to her, unable to see how in so many other ways she was being dragged down from her former wisdom into foolish thoughts and ways!

This leads to my second point about blessing or defilement and that it will change us. On the one hand, we struggle against defilement from *individuals*. On the other, we are beset by *corporate spiritual defilement* from our church, city, state, nation and the world. Our friend was being defiled not only by the lesbian individually; she was being overcome by the corporate spiritual defilement of the centuries-old stronghold of sodomy! These days the whole world is deluged by strongholds of sexual defilement — through television, movies, novels, porno magazines, etc., ad nauseam! Sometimes I think about the prophecy in Revelation 12:15, that the serpent would pour: "... water like a river out of his mouth after the woman, so that he might cause her to be swept away with the flood. . . ." One sure interpretation must be the Niagara of smut he has poured out of his mouth to sweep the church away in a flood of sexual defilements!

Every thought or action each of us does adds to or lightens the burden of defilement which sits upon us all! This means that every church service and every prayer meeting is an act of spiritual warfare, lifting some of the defilement of our age off us all. But it also means that there is no private sin, no matter how secret. Every sin adds to the epidemic of sin which now afflicts the church and all mankind.

In Genesis 20 we see that Abraham told Abimelech a half-lie. Fearing that he might be killed for the beauty of Sarah, he said she was his sister. In truth she was his half-sister. But he did not say she was his wife. When Abimelech took Sarah into his household, all the wombs of his household were closed. God then came to Abimelech in a dream and told him, "Behold, you are a dead man because of the woman whom you have taken, for she is married" (v.3). Note: this heathen king had sense enough to know that his sin could destroy his entire nation! — "Lord, wilt Thou slay a nation, even though blameless?" (v. 4) By "blameless," he meant that he had not yet been to bed with Sarah. God then told him that He had kept him from sinning against Himself and that if he would go to Abraham, *he* would pray for him and the wombs of his household would be opened again; and they were (vs. 6,7 & 17). *What one in authority does, even a heathen, either blesses or afflicts all his people.*

Now let us consider this: It is a known fact that certain presidents of the United States committed adultery while they were in the White House. (It is also true that President Lincoln participated in a seance in the White

House, and President Reagan was involved by his wife in astrology.) Add to this the lately revealed sins of so many Christian leaders. Is it a coincidence that this nation has been struck with a plague of sexual immorality? Defilement flows from leadership down.

When David, despite the resistance of his commander Joab, insisted upon taking a census of the people (1 Chron. 21), the seer Gad spoke for the Lord, saying that He would give David a choice: either three years of famine, three months to be swept away by his foes, or three days of the sword of the Lord slaying by pestilence (v. 12). David chose the latter and ". . .70,000 men of Israel fell"! (v. 14).

Korah, Dathan and Abiram (Num. 16) persuaded 250 discontented leaders to falsely claim to be priests. Fire from heaven burned up their censers and the earth opened its mouth and swallowed Korah, Dathan, Abiram and their families. But their actions had defiled the people who continued to grumble against Moses! The following morning, God told Moses, "Get away from among this congregation, that I may consume them instantly" (v. 46). Moses commanded Aaron to take his censer and run between God and the people, but before the plague could be checked, 14,700 died!

If the mere intention to sin, on the part of King Abimelech, sent an affliction upon all the wombs of his household, what greater afflictions are now descending upon America for the actual sins of its leaders?!!! I do not wish to lay blame on any president nor upon any Christian leaders.

Rather, I want to make all of us aware of the power of corporate spiritual defilement, and the ways it can work. Each of us is responsible to withstand and overcome whatever defilements may come from headship. *God is calling all Christians who understand these things to comprehend fully their corporateness and to intercede mightily in repentance!*

I believe the restoration of true corporate worship in these days is in part because God knows the intercessory power of all worship to erase defilement and bless mankind and the land.

Theological Defilements by Delusion

An example of theological defilement has already been discussed in the passage from *Healing the Wounded Spirit* quoted earlier. But I cannot close the subject without warning concerning two particular delusions rampant in the Body today.

The first is direct sexual spiritual defilement. Paula and I have ministered to many women who were convinced that the Lord Jesus came to them and made personal sexual love to them! A demon, posing as the Lord himself, told them that since they were now in fact the bride of Christ, one of the privileges and joys belonging to them by marital right was to have sex with him! The experience became so real, these women actually achieved orgasm. That kind of demon is called an *"incubus."*

We had to argue for hours with one woman who was absolutely certain that an incubus posing as the Lord loved her as no one else ever had. He alone had never deserted her. He was always there to comfort her when she needed him. She believed he only meant her well and was the best friend she had ever had. She remained reluctant to let him go, even after we finally convinced her that, rather than blessing her, he intended to drag her straight to hell!

A similar thing can happen to men. One man we ministered to awoke night after night to find that such a spirit had brought him to full erection and nearly to climax. A demon posing as a lovely female has caused some men, fully awake, to experience arousal so completely that they have reached climax, certain that they were actually having intercourse with an angelic being. That kind of demon is called a *"succubus."*

Deliverance is called for in such cases. But the victim will be able to withstand further incursions only if the counselor tracks down the vulnerability which originated in the person's life history. If the counselee does not come to *hate* the way the demon has used childhood woundings to defile him or her, the door will remain open for it to return. As in the case of the woman we dealt with for hours, many are defiled to such an extent that their thinking about the experience is a complete shambles. Patience and long, logical discussions may be required, or the result may be seven demons worse than the first (Luke 11:26)!

The second instance is a theological delusion rampant in the Body of Christ today. Years ago Paula and I saw it only occasionally throughout America. Recently it has reappeared, in a slightly different form, but nevertheless it is the same old trick of Satan.

The delusion says that at the same moment when God creates a man He has created a woman who is his "soul mate" or "spirit mate." This special person is *not* necessarily one's earthly spouse! The man or woman who finds his or her soul mate will feel "complete and whole." Anointing will vastly increase. Their prayers for each other (especially with laying on of hands) will exhilarate them beyond measure.

The deluded insist that this teaching is just for those "mature enough" to receive it. This is a "fresh and new revelation," released now that the Body contains the few mature ones who *can* receive it. Only the really mature could find their soul mates and experience such a distinctly "spiritual" relationship without disrupting their earthly married life.

Obviously, Satan's plan, in order to defile and destroy marriages, is to pander to the need in some to think of themselves as special and mature. The deception is as "new" as the first adultery recorded in the Bible! Paula and I first came across this deception in the early sixties. At present, a friend of ours in a nearby city is all caught up in this "new and exciting revelation." Her closest friends have been trying to make her see that it is truly a delusion, a doctrine of demons St. Paul prophesied about (1 Tim. 4:1). Her mind has been so defiled that the warnings and remonstrances only convince her that her friends are immature. Obviously, she cast her precious "pearls" before swine, and she can only feel sorry for these friends. They are going to miss out on the glory this teaching could have revealed, because they are so "backward and close-minded!" We are currently praying and confronting, in an effort to snatch ". . . from the fire" (Jude 23).

Satan has no new tricks. Even if this particular form of the delusion spreads no farther, the devil will dress it up in different clothes and trot it out at some later date and place. It grabs its victims by defilement, and panders to weaknesses in the flesh. It leads directly to spiritual adultery and, if unchecked, to separation and divorce. It separates its victims from long-held friendships and establishes new relationships with companions whose ears and hooves are growing at the same rate as Pinocchio's did!

Antidotes for Corporate Spiritual Defilement

The first and most powerful antidote for corporate spiritual defilement is that which was named earlier — *corporate worship.*

Other antidotes for corporate spiritual defilement include:

Intercessory groups formed especially to pray away the defilement over our land. During the Middle Ages, some monasteries existed specifically for that purpose.

Good and wholesome theater, movies, books, novels, stories, programs on TV, etc. Every time I watch a movie like "The Sound of Music," I feel cleansed and uplifted.

Wholesome humor. Watching such TV programs as Bill Cosby's "Himself" is therapeutic. It causes us to laugh at ourselves. Holy laughter breaks the spells of defilement.

Political moral consciousness. Pray that God will send men of unbending righteous principles onto the political scene and, if God so directs, to work in political organizations to make that happen (not to mention the potential for witness).

Antidotes for Individual Spiritual Defilement

1.) *Develop daily practices of spiritual hygiene.* Paula and

I simply pray each night that God will cleanse us from whatever may have latched on to our spirits, or entered in and defiled us during the day. We also offer "flash prayers" whenever we sense something unclean touching us.

2.) *Read the Word.* Hear Psalm 119:9-11:

How can a young man keep his way pure?
By keeping it according to Thy word.
With all my heart I have sought Thee;
Do not let me wander from Thy commandments.
Thy word I have treasured in my heart,
That I may not sin against Thee.

And Psalm 19:7-9a:

The law of the lord is perfect, restoring the soul;
The testimony of the Lord is sure, making wise the simple.
The precepts of the Lord are right, rejoicing the heart;
The commandment of the Lord is pure, enlightening the eyes.
The fear of the Lord is clean, enduring forever.

3.) *Devise alternate activities.* Play. Visit with family members about non-spiritual matters. Go for a walk. I used to take five or ten minutes between counselees to work in the garden, getting my hands into the good earth. I could feel the earth draining defilement out of me. Our Lord Jesus went to the mountaintops or into the wilderness to pray, when He could more easily have taken refuge in a nearby house.

4) *Keep communication and fulfilling sex going with your own mate; and pursue open sharing with others close to you.* Communication means more than talking. It means meeting heart-to-heart and spirit-to-spirit, exchanging ideas and emotions which leave one feeling lifted and refreshed. Wholesome sex leaves each spouse feeling good

about life and somehow refreshed and cleansed of defilement.

5.) *Observe the Sabbath.* Most servants of the Lord work hardest on Sunday. Keep another day inviolately as your day to rest. When defilement assails, it is tiredness which blurs our perceptive faculties.

6.) *Worship. Receive the sacrament of communion regularly.* Jesus said, "You are already clean because of the word which I have spoken to you" (John 15:3). Good sermons cleanse. But nothing washes our bodies and spirits better than receiving the body and blood of the Lord!

7.) *Be often among friends, and listen to them.* This is more than, and different from, the communication spoken of in number four. I mean playing games, being down to earth, laughing and teasing, joking and bantering, just living as a normal human being. *Enjoy life.* Don't let it get too serious.

8.) *Pray beforehand that the cross of Christ be firmly established between you and your counselee(s), and that the presence of the Lord will safeguard whatever transpires between you.*

9.) *Learn to distinguish between your own passions and those which come solely from defilement.* There is no shortcut to learning; wisdom comes by the route of experience. Listen to friends. Examine your feelings. After a while you will begin to discern empathetic defilement by its "strangeness." It somehow doesn't "fit." It doesn't "feel like you," as in the instance I shared at the beginning of the chapter, or the pediatrician and the choir director whose confused feelings and thoughts were so opposite to what they normally felt, or the case of the unattractive woman who nevertheless broadcast such a defiling sexual allurement. But beware; sometimes the defilement grabs precisely because it *does* feel like you.

In such instances, one must grow in the gift of discernment. But it will help if you maintain a stubborn reluctance not to act without counsel or outside the bounds of God's Word, and if you will have the humility to question constantly the source and veracity of your feelings and thoughts.

God has not given us infallible sensors and minds; we cannot always come to clear discernments. At those times, time is our ally, and haste is our enemy. Wait. Revelation will eventually come. Now, I most often catch it rather quickly, so that discerning empathetic defilement has become a valuable tool for getting more rapidly at what is in the heart of the other. But even so, I know better than to become overconfident — our Lord never said that involved ministry to others would ever be safe.

Empathetic defilement by itself is not temptation. One can be tempted only by one's own lusts (see James 1:14,15). Defilement becomes temptation when we believe its thoughts and feelings and add to them our own lusts and passions. For me, that realization became one of my sharpest tools for discerning what defilement was. I observed that defilement at first lacked the "fire power" of lustful passion. I saw that I only *thought* I wanted to do something, or *felt* like I did, *without the real urgency which would have been there had those thoughts and feelings been truly my own.*

After a bit of practice, one learns to sense when thoughts and feelings have come from outside oneself rather than from within, mainly by the lack of real "gut-churning" involvement — but you need to remember that this distinction vanishes, once you fully believe those thoughts and feelings and enlist your own passions into the situation.

Possible Cures

These are the same as those listed in the first chapter. You must beware lest your own perceptions become distorted by what is in those who are heavily into defilement. Be humble enough to check with others not close to the defiled, about what you feel led to do. Realize that if defilement and spiritual adultery have acted in tandem (and have hooked into unhealed dimensions of those to whom you minister), you are in for spiritual warfare. So get help. Don't be a "lone ranger." Back up the ministering team with prayer warriors not directly involved in the ministry. Persevere. It may be a long battle.

3

Attachments, Transferences, Affairs and Adultery

Attachments and transferences (taken together) are the third most common reason why some Christians commit adultery. *Attachment* happens when a person perceives subconsciously that he or she can be loved into more fulness of life through another and latches on to that one. *Transference* takes place in counseling when the counselee, having formed an attachment to the counselor, projects onto the counselor one or more unresolved relationships and tries to resolve them. The counselee then "loves" as though the counselor were his (or her) father or mother or brother/sister/friend/lost lover — whoever is the cause or object of whatever has not been resolved. The love is not real. It is composed first of projection, and then of gratitude.

Attachments and transferences happen to non-believers and Christians alike. Attachments can occur between *any* individuals. But *only* those who involve themselves deeply enough in one-on-one counseling are subject to transferences.

Attachments

Anyone, Christian or not, can become infatuated or enamored with another and want to spend inordinate amounts of time with the other person. Attachments are most frequently "one way" relationships: from one who wants or needs something toward another who is thought to be able to provide it. The "love" in those cases is composed mainly of admiration and hope. Occasionally attachment occurs both ways. In that case it can be called *philia* or brotherly love. Most marriages begin with attachment, and usually grow from there into *eros* (sexual and/or romantic love).

Attachments come into being for several reasons:

First, for friendship. We meet someone and something clicks inside. Either immediately or after several encounters, our spirit fastens on to the other. We "know in our knower" that we want more than mere acquaintanceship. If the other responds, our hearts are opened to inner bonding. We want to build long-term friendships. David and Jonathan experienced that kind of knitting of their souls: "Now it came about when he had finished speaking to Saul, that *the soul of Jonathan was knit to the soul of David, and Jonathan loved him as himself*" (1 Sam. 18:1).

In biblical times, if two decided to formalize such a bonding, they entered into a "blood covenant." A ceremony was held in which the friends cut their wrists and joined them within two rings of braided cloth, thoroughly bloodying the rings. Afterwards, both were to keep their rings as mementos of their bond (from which we derive our modern-day wedding rings). Next, a goat was slit down the middle and spread, legs pointing outwards, leaving space for a path between the halves. The two friends stood at either end of the animal and promised brotherhood. They then exchanged places, walking in a figure-eight pattern between the parts of the goat, signifying that they had now exchanged hearts of concern and were pledged to each other's blessing and prosperity. Then they traded cloaks and inserted each other's name into their own — from which practice women take their husbands' names (and in England many still retain hyphenated surnames). The covenant brothers had now become responsible for each other's lives and for their children and their children's children. The ceremony culminated in a "covenant meal," which by the "covenant of salt" (Num. 18:19) sealed their compact with each other. No relationship (other than marriage) was considered to be as sacred as that between blood brothers.

Our Lord himself performed the ritual of the blood covenant with Abram (Gen 15:12-21), passing between the pieces (v.17) in order to convince Abram of His faithfulness. Blood covenants are entered into between equals; but Abram had nothing to offer God, so God acted alone. His exchanging places with Abram was a foretype and promise of His exchanging places with us on the cross in our Lord Jesus Christ! The Lord returned to the covenant ceremony later on, changing Abram's name to Abraham by inserting His own name into Abram's (Gen. 17:5), "Abra — 'Yah' for 'Jahweh' — Am." Abra*ha*m thus became the "friend forever of God" (2 Chron. 20:7), and our Lord became known as the "covenant-making and covenant-keeping God."

So we see that attachments can be among the holiest of relationships! Nevertheless, they remain fraught with dangers. They can devolve into spiritual adultery with any friend, male or female. Too much time and attention may be given to friends who become that near and dear to us. In such close relationships, we are most liable to fall into idolatry. Obviously, attachments to members of the opposite sex can tempt us beyond spiritual adultery into the physical act.

We learn balance and wisdom in life only through experience, but sometimes that experience is laden with unnecessary pain. Ignorance of attachments and their power can expose many to perplexing addictions to out-of-balance relationships, to hurtful confusions and to multiple kinds of sinful experiences! Paula and I have counseled many whose relationships began merely as attachments designed by God for friendship and blessing, but which evolved into blighted marriages and nightmarish adulteries.

The second kind of attachment is for learning.

During my college years, the most influential man in my life was Rabbi Ernest Jacobs, who had fled from Nazi Germany and subsequently became a professor at Drury College. Under his tutelage, I studied European,

English and Old Testament histories, a course on prophets, and second-and-third-year German. My spirit "leaped" when I met him. I hung on his every word, in and out of class. I had attached to him to drink every draught of knowledge I could from him.

The same thing happened when I met Winston Nunes of Canada. I sought to be with him every moment. A wise old proverb says, "If you find a man of wisdom, let your foot wear out his threshold."

Many parishioners latch onto their pastors in the same way. Not only is attaching for learning permissible, but the Lord advises it: "The mouth of the righteous flows with wisdom..." (Prov. 10:31a), and "He who walks with wise men will be wise..." (Prov. 13:20a). However, we do need to walk circumspectly, lest we idolize another person or be led astray. Deuteronomy 13:1-4 can be applied as well to pastors and teachers as to prophets:

> If a prophet or a dreamer of dreams arises among you and gives you a sign or a wonder, and the sign or the wonder comes true, concerning which he spoke to you, saying, 'Let us go after other gods (whom you have not known) and let us serve them,' you shall not listen to the words of that prophet or that dreamer of dreams; for the Lord your God is testing you to find out if you love the Lord your God with all your heart and with all your soul. You shall follow the Lord your God and fear Him; and you shall keep His commandments, listen to His voice, serve Him, and cling to Him.

The Lord expects us to use our own minds to discern whether what we hear leads us closer to Him and His righteousness, or farther away to destruction.

And He expects us to stand on our own two feet. Some have entered into *intellectual spiritual idolatry,* forsaking the Lord and their own God-given minds for the mentality of someone they admired too much. Early in our ministry, Paula and I used to see what we called "camp followers," intellectually idolatrous people who showed up at every meeting, ostensibly seeking knowledge. We soon discovered that no matter how much teaching they heard, they retained little and never matured. "For among them are those who enter into households and captivate weak women weighed down with sins, led on by various impulses, *always learning and never able to come to the knowledge of the truth*" (2 Tim. 3:6-7). Many of these "weak women" turned out to be weak men!

It is possible to turn any of God's blessings to loss and destruction. Some fall into trouble because they don't understand that attachments, even for learning, can progress by ignorance and confusion into spiritual and even physical adulteries.

The third kind of attachment is for leeching. "The leech has two daughters, 'Give,' 'Give.' " (Prov. 30:15a). Leeches are people who don't discipline themselves to keep their spirits abiding in Christ; they maintain a superficial sense of well-being by attaching to other Christians. They draw upon others' energies in much the same way as leeches suck the blood of unwary waders and swimmers.

Paula and I, being natural burden-bearers, at one time were nearly bled to utter exhaustion by dozens of spiritual leeches! Having swallowed the lie (due to our inflated sense of self-importance) that they would achieve wholeness only by our carrying them, we were reluctant to give up and let them go. Finally, we realized the hard way that leeches have *no intention of becoming whole.* They want to be carried for as long as anyone will endure them. When at last we could hear, the Lord showed us Psalm 118:12, "They swarmed around me like bees, but they died out as quickly as burning thorns; *in the name of the Lord I cut them off*" (NIV). By then we had learned that sometimes God's kindness has to be expressed in ways that seem ruthless. We prayed fervently, cutting loose every leech who had attached to us. To our surprise, not only did *we* feel lighter and freer, *many of them got free* and began to stand on their own. Allowing them to latch on had not helped them at all; it had only hindered them.

Paula and I have come upon many servants of the Lord who are staggering around in "third stage burn-out," unaware that leeches have drained them dry. When that used to happen to me, I felt emptied of all compassion, "cored out," — as though I couldn't muster one more gracious humane response to anyone! I felt as though there were a hole in my chest, crying for someone to fill it up again with human sensitivity. When a servant has been so ravaged, he or she becomes vulnerable to anyone who might seem to offer comfort and "re-fueling." Had I not been determinedly moral and true to Paula, and had I been unable at the time to find and receive help at home, I could have been swept away by any woman who would have offered to hold me and restore my heart! I have grieved for the many brothers of the cloth who were unaware of what was impelling them into spiritual and physical adulteries. They fell because they were drained by leeches and comforted by others, just when they found themselves blocked out from refreshment at home!

The fourth kind of attachment is distinctly sexual. No matter how spiritually mature we may become, we all remain susceptible to certain individuals, whose powerful "chemistry" attracts us physically. Whoever thinks he has spiritually matured beyond the possibility of sexual attachments is fooling himself. A woman to whom I once ministered was so old and so mature in Christ, I thought she surely could not have entertained any sexual feelings toward me — or anyone else! But years later I discovered that she had been plagued continually by sexual dreams and waking fantasies about me. Then I understood why I, who had thought myself beyond such things, had been perplexed to find occasional sexual thoughts toward her running through my mind! I had never thought of empathetic defilement as I would have with a younger woman, because I never suspected that someone her age could have had such feelings.

Sexual chemistry can lure the uninformed and unwary into unwise attachments and spiritual and physical adulteries. Somehow we have come to think that what we feel emotionally and physically is honest and real. Nothing could be further from the truth! Emotional feelings are always subject to carnality and confusions. They come from the heart, which is desperately corrupt and wicked (Jer. 17:9). Physical feelings may be real, but too often our corrupt hearts, rather than our renewed minds in Christ, interpret their meanings. Far too many have fallen because they believed sexual allurements were born of real love.

The final kind of attachment is due to "spiritual kinship." There are some whom we somehow recognize immediately as "family." We feel as though we must have come from the same family in heaven: "For this reason, I bow my knees before the Father, from whom *every family in heaven* and on earth derives its name. . ." (Eph. 3:14&15). Whether or not there is in fact such a thing as being of the same heavenly family, our spirit leaps in recognition and whispers to our mind, "Stay by this one. This is family."

That kind of attachment can become any or all of the other four — friendship, learning, leeching or sexual affinity. In itself, spiritual kinship is neither good nor bad. What we do with it can be. All five forms of attachment may lead to spiritual adultery, affairs and physical adultery. Each may also grow into transference, if we become deeply involved in trying to help the other.

The Debacle of Marriages Born in Transference

Many pastors, and a few otherwise well-trained counselors, know virtually nothing about transference. If that ignorance is coupled with vulnerability in the counselor, great damage can result. Paula and I have ministered to many who, because of transferences, became enmeshed in "sticky" relationships. They thought their client's love for them was real and responded in kind. These relationships then became affairs, most of which ended in physical adulteries.

All relationships based on need are intrinsically

unstable. Quite apart from transference, if a man marries an emotional child or a woman marries a "boy," most often what lies behind the relationship is the need of the one to "parent," and the hunger of the other to be parented. In many such unions, the parenting partner tires of that role, or the "child" begins to grow up. Habitual ways of relating must then be brought to death, and new ones built. Usually one and sometimes both are unable to adjust, and the marriage shatters.

Transferences embody immaturity seeking maturity, weakness wanting strength, or emotional sickness drinking health. Whatever the components, *neediness is the base upon which all transference relationships are built.*

Some "unwise" marriages do survive; either the participants become frozen in their roles or they adjust to changes. But such marriages and transferences have one crucial difference: *Marriage is not entered into with change as its primary object, but transferences exist for that very purpose.* This means that if a counselor believes his client's feelings for him are true mate-love and responds in kind, he dooms his lover to disappointment. The love they share cannot successfully become marital. Mate-love is born of mutual trust and respect, between co-equals. Transference-love is by definition dependent and delusive.

Paula and I have often counseled those who actually divorced their spouses to marry their transferees. We have yet to hear of any who made a successful transition! One would think transference-love could die and true mate-love could be born in its place. But it never happens that way. Need relationships don't engender the same kind of respect, admiration and trust that equality creates.

It is not long before the client discovers she (or he) is not really in love with the pastor/counselor. Time and growing maturity begin to reveal that what seemed to be love was in fact mere projection and idealistic admiration. Projection in this instance means that out of unrecognized need for a father or mother, the younger one has projected onto the older that he/she will fulfill not only that need, but many subconscious expectations, both positive and negative. The younger one is actually working through unresolved issues and finding the long-lost love of one or both parents. When that kind of love fades (is no longer needed), disillusionment sets in. Normally, the pastor/counselor is considerably older, and when the cold light of reality dispels the fog of confusion, the younger partner finds herself (himself) locked into what has now become a distasteful marital relationship. Ordinarily, there remain tender feelings of loyalty and some admiration, but the disappointed one can't help but see that these are not the appropriate feelings of true mate-love — and they never were.

The younger spouse now finds herself (himself) looking around, seeing other desirable people closer to her (his) own age. Guilt floods in, but he or she can't stop the looking. Eventually the former counselee realizes that whatever tiny flame of mate-love may have flickered for a moment is now extinguished.

This picture may seem too deterministic, and, human nature being what it is, there are variations. Probably some do survive the adjustments. Paula and I know of some marriages which lasted — through duty to the children or their determination not to divorce again — but the spark is gone! The two now only mark time until the grave. They are not growing together as a team into the wholeness and gracious mellowness found in so many who celebrate their fortieth, fiftieth and sixtieth anniversaries.

A young woman we knew went to her pastor for counseling. She needed a "father." From the honeymoon on, her husband had revealed himself to be an insensitive boor. The pastor had run dry in his own marital relationship. The young woman soon entered into spiritual adultery towards him, which rapidly became transference. As she worked through the unhealed areas in her childhood concerning her father and other family members, the pastor's abundant compassion never failed to calm her tempestuous emotions. With every session, her "love" for him increased.

Meanwhile, as her desire to have a husband like him

defiled his heart, the pastor's mind translated that as his own desire to have a wife as lovely as she. His failures at home had so parched the ground of his heart that her obvious love for him became like a delightfully refreshing rain. He began to look forward not only to their counseling appointments but also to church functions she might be expected to attend. He found himself watching the way she moved, "feeling" her rhythms inside himself almost as if he were one with her. He discovered himself wincing at mental images of her husband embracing her. Having a pastor's heart, he at first ascribed those to his concern that such a clumsy, insensitive oaf could only trample her feelings and bruise her body. He was unaware that he was actually agonizing over her with the jealousy of a thwarted lover.

So far, this could be the story of countless transferences which become double. Double or counter-transferences occur whenever a counselor is defiled into believing the "love" and returns it, also unconsciously working out unhealed areas. Doubles always hook into hidden areas in each heart, sparking almost irresistible fires of attraction.

Most double transferences proceed rather quickly beyond spiritual into physical adultery. This one did, and the man lost his church, and his wife and family. Some counselors, like the righteous pastor written of earlier, flee from such dangerous relationships. But very, very few escape! Some realize they are in danger but hang in there because they are afraid that, if they withdraw, the counselee will not be able to take yet another devastating rejection. Duty and self-importance thus blind them to their own imminent destruction.

Paula and I have ministered to some who ended up seducing their pastor/counselor because of unrecognized double transferences. One such woman had slept with her priest and then complained bitterly that if she were to be damned for sin, she ought at least to have been allowed to enjoy it! (His unrescinded vow of celibacy had rendered him impotent!)

Transference-related adulteries, separations and divorces have shattered an incredible number of homes and churches! Surely God's people are being "destroyed for lack of knowledge."

Symptoms of Single Transferences

The symptoms are identical to those for spiritual adultery and defilement, plus:

1) The counselee *thinks too highly of the counselor* — "You are the only one who truly understands me."

2) *The client covertly or openly asks for a "special relationship."* One beautiful parishioner, apparently not consciously intending to be seductive, several times said to me, "John, I don't know what I want from you, but I know I just want to be 'special' to you." She had been raped as a teenager, and her father had blamed *her*! Unconsciously, she wanted to be as a daughter to me, though she was nearly my own age.

3) *The counselee begins to "cook up" problems.* The counselor may suspect the counselee wants to feel loved more than to get well.

(It should be noted that this and most of the other symptoms could be rightly attributed to factors other than transference. Diagnosis always requires discernment. It could be harmful to leap to false conclusions.)

4) *The counselee may invite the counselor to social occasions, wanting to be more than just another "project."* The client wants to become a close personal friend (similar to item 2, but in this case a specific request for friendship).

5) *The counselee exhibits typical signs of infatuation* — longing looks, "innocent" touches, unintended double-entendre words, etc.

Symptoms of Double Transferences

1) *Inordinate desire in the counselor to be the sole healer;* (playing God).

2) *The counselor finds himself/herself wanting to give more and longer sessions than problems warrant.*

3) *The counselee's needs and temperament too snugly*

fit the counselor's skills — and vulnerabilities. Beware when the counselor starts noticing how "ideal" he or she is to be that person's helper — perhaps the only one "who can really understand."

4) *Isolation. The counselor begins to seek more privacy than the office affords:* "Someone might overhear confidential matters." Never mind that the office has been perfectly acceptable for other counseling. If someone points that out, the response is apt to be, "But this is a special case, requiring more sensitivity to confidentiality."

5) *Stronger, more emotional feelings of "love" in the counselor than* agape *(God's love) or* philia *(brotherly love) warrant.* Eros *(romantic love) begins to send signals in dreams and unbidden waking fantasies.*

6) *Breakdowns in communication, prayers and sex life at home,* coupled with the beginnings of unfavorable comparisons of the spouse to the counselee.

7) *Inability to hear friends' warnings, and aggressive defensiveness.*

8) *Fear deep within the spirit and vague senses of being betrayed* (though no betrayer can be identified). Actually, the counselor senses his or her own wrongness and that of the relationship but is incapable of facing the truth of his or her deception. So he projects his apprehensions outward until he appears paranoid to other people, who wonder, "What's happening to him?"

9) *Feelings within the counselor of being unprotected and somehow exposed,* at the same moment that the counselor feels expansive and ultra-protective toward the counselee. These anxieties are in fact born of his/her spirit's fear that he/she may be in deception after all, and if so, "Where was God?" Plus the gnawing fear, if sinful actions have already taken place, that someone will realize what's going on and tell others.

10) *The onset of compulsive behaviors.* For example, inability to resist phoning the other "to see if everything's alright," or to stop thinking about the "lover," or to control, or at least limit, the burgeoning habit of daydreaming ("what if. . ." "maybe we could have. . .").

Antidotes And Remedies

1) *In your own way, purge your hidden motivations with your spouse (or friend, if not married), as Paula and I prayed about any possible sinful sexual factors in my heart* (first pages, first chapter).

2) But add a further dimension: BECOME TRANSPARENT. *Let Christ's love shine through you.* Transference is a psychological dynamic which occurs frequently in secular counseling and less frequently in Christian counseling. But it does not need to happen at all in Christian counseling! Transference is a worldly copy of true Christian counseling. Lacking the indwelling power of the Holy Spirit, a secular counselor can give only human love, which necessarily attaches the counselee to the counselor. But because a Christian learns how to love in Christ and not in the flesh, counselees (or anyone receiving ministry from any Christian) can move quickly beyond fleshly attachments and come to know the fulness of our Lord Jesus Christ.

After Paula and I had brought to death on the cross whatever in my flesh might cause people to become hung up, many easily found their healing in Jesus. Full transferences didn't happen anymore. But some persisted in latching on to me despite all our prayers. The Lord answered our cry by saying, "John, the reason is that your presence promises My love, but your fear of involvement blocks it. They can't get to Me because of your unbelief. Now that you have brought those things to death, believe that it is I Who am loving these people to life through you. Let go, trust Me, and love them freely. It will be My love they receive." Paradoxically, when I then began to express the love I had feared lest it trip people up on me, people truly received my love as His love and attached cleanly to Jesus alone!

It is continuous death on the cross which creates transparency. Whenever I sense that counselees are not getting cleanly through me to Jesus, I return to the foot of the cross to say, "Okay, Lord, what of my flesh is hanging out now? Why can't people get through to you?

Bring me to death again, Lord. Remake me transparent."

For those needing ministry, death on the cross is never sufficient of itself to accomplish healing and transformation. Christians need to experience resurrection as well. They must come to life in areas that never functioned before, or they will fall back to the familiar. Sometimes our Lord sovereignly performs resurrections — instantly, it seems. But frequently, for His own purposes, He chooses to love people to life *through* His servants. If we are not sufficiently dead to self, that's where ministry gets sticky.

> In a large house there are articles not only of gold and silver, but also of wood and of clay; some are for noble purposes and some for ignoble. *If a man cleanses himself from the latter, he will be an instrument for noble purposes, made holy, useful to the Master and prepared to do any good work.*
>   (2 Tim. 2:20-21, NIV)

Since Paula and I learned these things, no one has entered into transference toward us. But we have hundreds of whole and happy spiritual sons and daughters around the world! (See Chapter 21, "Fathers and Mothers in Christ," in our book, *The Transformation of the Inner Man.)*

3) *Learn to say the "Abraham-Isaac prayer" regularly.* Everyone's ministry becomes his Isaac. If we do not put our ministry on the altar, it will have us! The Lord will possess neither our ministry nor us. Flesh will impel all our service. *Our* ministry, rather than Jesus, will become the god we serve. We will then mistake fleshly zeal for anointing and worldly insights for gifts of knowledge and perception. When that happens, we can't be transparent. People will fasten on to us rather than Jesus. In our fleshly zeal and self-importance, we will then minister carnally, trying ourselves to be their saviors and re-creators.

The Abraham-Isaac prayer is simply, "I place my ministry (name it — counseling, music, teaching, evangelizing, preaching, helping — whatever) on the altar, Lord. I give it back to You. Slay its hold upon me. Set me free from it. Henceforth it is Yours, not mine."

If we do not repeat this prayer regularly, we will lose our transparency. We will then "work" gimmicks, fleshly methods, personal programs from a hidden agenda, and emotional "trips" on all we minister to. For example, if the Lord gives me a new insight while counseling the first person of the day and I don't remember immediately to put it on the altar, the next several counselees will have that problem — whether or not that is in fact their problem! (I'm "into that" today. It has me.)

4) *Release.* If improper attachments have begun, *cut free.* Release those people emotionally, intellectually and spiritually.

5) If prayers won't do it, act in wisdom and righteousness. Counselors must act to protect themselves and their counselees, and friends must act to deliver both from error. How?

A) *Invite a fellow counselor into the sessions.*

B) *Avoid becoming companions outside the office.* A counseling ministry we know had to let a staff counselor go because she was becoming too friendly and familiar with her counselees — taking them out to eat far too often, for example. While we do need to be friendly, the counseling relationship must be kept strictly professional, as much as possible.

C) *Share with your spouse what can be discreetly discussed.* Don't name names. Inform the spouse that people are attempting to latch on, and pray through your weaknesses in the flesh again — together.

D) *Realize* that once a counselee has fastened on in the flesh, a counselor may not be able for a time to transfer the counselee purely to Jesus. The counselor may have to walk it through. A wise counselor invites others to help, explains to the counselee what transference relationships are, and girds for the "long haul."

6) *Get perspective.* Don't let this one counseling situation overshadow every other. Reduce its importance. Talk it over with your spouse, but then forget it. If transference has become double, that may be impossible alone. Every counselor, therefore, needs friends who are his personal iconoclasts, who can help him smash his "idols" through wholesome play and companionship.

7) *Recognize when the job is done.* When the other is capable of standing alone, let go. A counselor's task is akin to St. Paul's ". . . with whom I am again in labor until Christ is formed in you" (Gal. 4:19). Until the other can walk free in Christ, counselors carry in the heart (Phil. 1:7). The difficulty is to know how and when to release. Counselors must be careful not to release transferees too soon, lest early withdrawal be received as rejection and cause relapses.

Therefore, symptoms of readiness are:

A) *Feistiness.* The counselee begins to pick fights with the counselor, like a teenager wanting to "cut the apron strings."

B) *Courage.* The counselee stands and takes hold of life for herself (or himself).

C) *Assertiveness* has become standard and appropriate to situations.

D) *Equanimity.* The "yo-yo effect" has ended. There are no more wild ups and downs. The counselee stands without strain.

E) *The counselee knows himself (herself), recognizes "games" quickly and easily stops them.*

F) *The counselee says, "I'm not in love with you, am I!"* (This is a statement, not a question). The counselee has returned to balance and is declaring independence.

8) Finally, *every counselor needs to be submitted to authority.* If superiors advise breaking it off or enlisting a partner, let counselors obey with alacrity and a willing spirit. Counselors should above all else shun pride and

presumption, and remember that they are not the only nor the best counselors God has for their counselees. "I planted the seed, Apollos watered it, but God made it grow. *So neither he who plants nor he who waters is anything, but only God, who makes things grow*" (1 Cor. 3:6-7, NIV).

4

Fornication, Affairs And Adultery

Clarification of Terms

Fornication occurs when an *unmarried man* and an *unmarried woman* engage in sexual intercourse.

Adultery is when a *married man* and a *married woman* have sexual intercourse but they are not married to each other.

If an *unmarried person* has intercourse with someone who is *married, the first commits fornication, the second, adultery.*

Some Christians have tried to tell us the words "fornication" and "adultery" are identical in meaning and apply only to married people. They therefore conclude that if unmarried persons engage in sexual intercourse, no sin is involved! How any sincere Christian could believe such nonsense is beyond me! "Or do you not know that the unrighteous shall not inherit the kingdom of God? Do not be deceived; neither *fornicators*, nor idolaters, nor *adulterers...*" (1 Cor. 6:9). If those two words (fornicators and adulterers) mean the same, one is redundant and thus meaningless. And how can they miss Exodus 22:16 and Deuteronomy 22:28-29, both of which say that if a man seduces a virgin he must marry her? Verse 29 adds, "*...because he has violated her*; he cannot divorce her all his days."

Scripturally there is no escape — sexual intercourse before marriage is sin! Some people merely want to twist Scripture to justify their sinful desires. Every Christian should set himself as St. Paul did: "...we have renounced the things hidden because of shame, not walking in craftiness or adulterating the word of God, but by the

79

manifestation of truth commending ourselves to every man's conscience in the sight of God" (2 Cor. 4:2).

Fornication has become an epidemic in our society. In my youth, the young woman who had lost her virginity before the wedding night was a rarity. Today the girl who has kept hers is even more rare! Some surveys have reported that at least 80% of America's teenagers have already become "sexually active" — today's euphemism for "sexually sinful."

In the second section of this book, I will explain more fully the historical, theological and cultural causes for the increase of sexual sinfulness in our day. Here I want to list some of the societal causes which make it difficult for our youth to keep out of fornication.

Societal Causes for Fornication

The foremost cause of fornication among young Christians today is peer pressure. Demands to conform are enormous. Teenagers and young adults have often told Paula and me: "Boyfriends tell us if we don't 'put out' we'll never get another date." "We don't get invited to parties." "No one likes us." "If our friends find out we're still virgins, they call us 'chicken,' 'silly prudes,' 'stuck-up,' 'holier-than-thou.' "

It is a powerful drive in teenagers to be popular. Some Christians manage to remain popular and "straight," but these are few and far between. Most Christian teenagers who insist on being moral are often consigned to rejection and loneliness. The choice is painfully obvious — succumb or suffer.

The second major societal reason is "Everyone's doing it." I am not referring here to peer pressure but to the numbing effect of the flood of movies, TV shows, novels, short stories, and to the bad examples set by some "Christian" leaders. By far the most destructive of the "everyone's-doing-it" pressures is the example of parents. Separations, divorces, dates brought home, sexual activities of parents with illicit partners witnessed or sensed, all these erode the virtue of fidelity in young minds. Children of shattered or unfaithful homes, without the intervention of God, cannot sustain life-long bonding and fidelity.

Paula and I grew tired of our children keeping company with what we called "the orangutans." We said, "Why don't you find some kids from healthy, stable homes to run with?"

They responded, "But, Mom, Dad, there aren't any. Everyone in our class is from a broken home!" We checked and found that in fact ours were among the very few children in their entire school who were not from one-parent or divorced and/or remarried families! Our community was, sad to say, not that different from most in America and Canada. Teachers everywhere report much the same statistics to us: more than half the class usually come from broken homes. Children raised in such families have not seen lifetime commitment demonstrated, nor the holiness of sexuality confined to one partner for life. Moreover, they refrain from making any real commitments; the pain of broken relationships in childhood has caused them to fear to risk. They choose to protect themselves by relating only superficially and conditionally. The blessedness of constancy and even of morality has not been written on their hearts by experience, and they are totally unequipped to participate in real intimacy in which they meet, know, become one with, and cherish another.

By contrast, moral parents who stay happily married produce moral offspring who also stay happily married. All four of our sons are confirmed one-woman men. Our son Mark gladdened our hearts recently when a sexually immoral scene flashed on the TV screen. He winced, and said, "I can't even *think* of giving my body to a woman other than Maureen without a shudder of revulsion!" I feel the same way, and so did my father — which is of course why our sons do. Our two daughters have the same determination to be moral and true.

The third societal cause of fornication is the erosion of belief in the absoluteness of moral law and in the holiness of marital sex in our day. When I was a teenager, it was the thing to do to park and "pet" or "neck" or "smooch." It was also just as normal for sexual passions to become overly aroused. Sexual passions raced like a runaway freight train! But for most of us, the sense of the awesome absoluteness of God's commands and of His discipline quickly dampened our ardor. I can remember becoming "hot and bothered" and then being sweetly cooled off by the grace of God as He recalled His laws to my mind. Awareness of God's call for sanctity in marital sex would then grow within me and quench my fires like an automatic sprinkler.

> How can a young man keep his way pure? By living according to your word... I have hidden your word in my heart that I might not sin against you.
>
> (Ps. 119:9 & 11, NIV)

> For wisdom will enter your heart, And knowledge will be pleasant to your soul; Discretion will guard you, Understanding will watch over you, To deliver you from the way of evil. . . .
>
> (Prov. 2:10-12a)

Today, the fear of God is gone! Our young people are not guarded by holy respect for His discipline. The Word no longer resonates in their hearts, warding off evil. Their minds may know the Law, but lack of sacrificial living has meant that the Word has not been written onto their hearts. Instead, they have been raised in a "gimme-gimme" age characterized by selfish gratification — and, for all too many, by the absolute conviction that it's their God-given right to have whatever seems to please at the moment.

The fourth societal cause is the lack of meaningful chores in childhood. Few today would advocate doing away with our many labor-saving devices. Thank God that automatic dishwashers, clothes washers and driers, microwave ovens and the like have liberated women from lives of drudgery. But the flip side of that benefit is that our children have grown up feeling useless!

In my childhood, chores were necessary for survival. Today, chores, if they are assigned at all, seem to be mere busywork. If I didn't milk the cows, their bawling woke the family and all the neighbors. If I didn't tend to the chickens and weed the garden, we didn't eat! Getting up early on freezing mornings to milk and do chores was painful. Summers, I learned the value and the virtue of sacrifice by forcing myself to weed while sweat made mud streaks down my face. I learned to love labor for others. More to the point of our discussion, I learned to cherish others' property. I knew firsthand the sacrifices everyone endured in those Depression days of the thirties to obtain whatever possessions they had.

Most of our children have never been taught the virtue of sacrificial labor for others. Things have been given to them so plentifully that they have little or no sense of the value of what belongs to another. Most modern movies aimed at teenagers portray casual destruction of property, wanton disregard for others, and "heroes" getting away with behavior that in real life would land them in jail. Is it any wonder such attitudes carry over into what young people think about their bodies and the bodies of others?! It takes enormous self-sacrificial determination to halt the onslaughts of mounting sexual passions. Most modern children have never been asked to pour themselves out for others until the vital skills of self-sacrifice could become ingrained. Rather, they have been taught to expect that whatever they want, they ought to receive — and if they don't, something is wrong with their parents!

Before I met Paula, there were two young women I was serious about. There were evenings with each of them when sexual desires were nearly unstoppable. There were times when excitement overran the checks of the Spirit in my spirit. All that kept me virginal was the awareness that this delightful creature whose kisses had become "sweeter than wine" might not become my wife, and I had no right to defraud my brother of his glory (1 Thess. 4:6). More powerfully upon my conscience, I had no right to possess what had not yet been given to me by God. That wisdom was placed in my heart by those hours of sacrificial labor for the family. I knew in the very core of my being the cost of and respect for what belongs to another. When I testify to young people today of my experiencing respect for others' property as a powerful sexual deterrent, most smile politely — and some cannot suppress chuckling! To them, my thoughts on this subject seem hopelessly out-of-date, irrelevant and even naive! That way of thinking is so non-existent for them, they believe I am only fooling myself!

My upbringing was not an isolated case. We know of a family of parents and seven children who have struggled for years to survive on their farm. Each child has had to work, long and hard. The contribution of each has been necessary to all. The father's brother is a professional man whose income has enabled him to provide every conceivable convenience for his wife and every desired possession for their children. They have taken their children to Hawaii and many other vacation spots around the world. The farmer and his wife have home-schooled their children to save money and have never been able to take their children on such trips.

Recently the professional brother's family visited the farm. As they drove away, the parents were stunned to hear their children complaining, "I wish we had a life like theirs on the farm. Our lives are so *boring!*" How typical this sentiment is! Young people want to contribute — they want their existence to mean something. They respond readily to the challenge of Youth With a Mission, or the

Peace Corps. They want to sacrifice by giving to others. If they lack that chance, they destroy themselves and others in senseless acquisition, especially sexual.

The fifth cause of fornication I see among Christians today is availability of opportunity. When I was a youngster, we were not allowed to be alone with the opposite sex, except under carefully guarded circumstances. No college man was ever allowed in women's dorms, unless it was Open House Day. Curfew hours for women were strict. Severe penalties were dealt out for infractions. At home, dad and mom were just upstairs within earshot, and at curfew time they would call out, "Good night, young man!", or blink the lights.

Few of us had our own cars, and when we could get dad's car for the night and drive out to park, police would come by regularly, shining flashlights at us and making us move on. We lived in fear of discovery — even when we were alone, who knew when someone might show up?! Today, on most college campuses, no supervision exists at all. Co-ed dorms are the norm in many universities, and men are allowed in women's rooms any hour of the day or night.

Even after Paula and I were married, we had a hard time convincing motel owners to let us have a room — we had to show ID's to prove we were married! Today's young people can easily whisk off to hiding places — a secluded spot in the woods (where police no longer check on them), a friend's place, or practically any motel.

Parents in our day possessed a keener sense of duty to guard the young from themselves. Immoral young men feared to trifle with the daughters of fiercely protective Christian fathers. Even non-Christian parents could almost always be counted on to keep a watchful eye. Today, that sense of duty has evaporated at the very time when opportunity has reached almost unlimited bounds. Many parents leave their children alone at home for days at a time.

The sixth cause is the availability and reliability of contraceptives. When we were young, the pill was non-existent. Diaphragms had only just been invented and no way could an unmarried person get one (they had to be fitted by physicians, and none would). Condoms were notorious for tearing or coming off.

We could not escape the haunting fear of pregnancy. (Abortion was out of the question, even if it had been legal.) Being pregnant meant you were "hooked" for life, and fathers would insist on a wedding — if necessary, at the business-end of a shotgun! Since paternity could not be proven in those days, some unscrupulous men would "ditch" girls to suffer shame and disgrace, which strengthened a young woman's resolve to say "No!" But today, even some Christian parents think it their duty to provide condoms or the pill!

Today's young people are more informed about hygiene. They know — or think they know — how to avoid getting diseases. In my youth, many young people with immoral urges were frightened into celibacy by fear of sexual diseases. Today, even the onslaught of the dreaded killer AIDS deters only a few. Many misguided parents think they are protecting their children from gonorrhea, syphilis, herpes and AIDS by teaching them about condoms; whereas, in fact, they may be only encouraging them to be immoral.

Which leads us to the seventh cause: It has been documented that where Planned Parenthood and school sex education classes have been active, fornication and unwanted pregnancies have dramatically increased! Planned Parenthood now gives "greeting cards" to high school youth, with condoms affixed to the inner page! They even offer condoms in varying styles and colors — for free! (This material has been taken from an open letter written by Alana Myers to Beverly La Haye and sent by her to the churches in the summer of 1988. Beverly La Haye, Concerned Women for America, 122 "C" Street, NW, Suite 800, Washington, DC 20001).

The liberal mentality often perceives a problem and then, with foolish zeal, provides absolutely the wrong answers! For example, we have the problem of women caught in unwanted pregnancies. Instead of insisting on chastity among the unmarried, and teaching about good contraceptives to the married, liberals lobby for laws and vote huge funds so that women can murder the unwanted lives within them — to the tune of more than 16,000,000 abortions (in America alone) at this writing! Or, there is the problem of more and more young people becoming "sexually active." Rather than lobby for funds to eradicate pornography, rather than teach the value and rewards of righteous behavior and warn of the destructive consequences of sexual immorality, liberals obtain $30,000,000 from the U.S. government to provide condoms, and teach young people how to have immoral sex *safely!* (La Haye, op. cit.) This is quite a bit like seeing a forest fire, but instead of calling in men and equipment to fight the fire, everybody gets torches and cans of gasoline so they can set "safe" fires!

The eighth cause, most telling and cruel, is molestation or involvement in sexual stimulation far too early in life. Paula's book, *Healing Victims of Sexual Abuse,* sadly chronicles the effects of molestation, especially in the chapter, "The Depths of Devastation." I'll not repeat that material here, except to say that Paula reports again and again that girls who are molested often become promiscuous.

(Though sexual molestation and too-early stimulation are obviously very personal, I list them under societal causes in order to indicate that today family structures have so crumbled that the resultant problems are not sporadic but epidemic throughout our society.)

We have found that if parents leave their children too long in bed with them, or in the same room where the sounds and odors of sexual activity can stimulate the children, the young ones are adversely affected. They become sexually aroused before they have the understanding, maturity or social skills to handle their feelings. "Daughters of Jerusalem, I charge you by the gazelles and by the does of the field: Do not arouse or awaken love until it so desires" (Song of Songs 2:7, NIV).

Whatever the correct exegesis of that verse may be, certainly a valid *rhema* meaning for any parent is: "Don't expose your infants and young children to sexually stimulating experiences." Children should not be allowed to see explicitly sexual scenes, either between parents or in movies or on TV or anywhere else. We have counseled children whose too early exposure manifested itself in attempts to imitate intercourse with playmates, fondling of their own and others' genital organs, crude and offensive language, addiction to pornography and voyeurism and, of course, sexual promiscuity in teen-age and infidelity in marriage. The list of sexual difficulties and aberrations stemming from early exposure is almost endless.

Affection between parents should be seen as often as possible. But sexual arousal should be shared between husband and wife only behind closed doors. Nor should nudity or immodesty be allowed in front of the children, especially those of the opposite sex. My mother carefully taught me that sex is private because it is holy, and reserved for a married couple. I saw or heard nothing other than modesty, though my parents were deeply romantic and greatly in love, especially in my early years.

My father was very affectionate to my mother in our presence, but I never saw a sexual touch or heard a suggestive remark or off-color jest. Sex was treated at all times in our home as something private and very holy and good. *For young people there is no better antidote to sexual temptation than parental example.* Obviously, there is nothing more adversely affective than the sins and improprieties parents engage in. Too few parents are aware of that today and so fail to give up their own selfish desires for the sake of their children's wholesome upbringing and healthy sexual attitudes — with consequent dire results.

The moral standards and safeguards which guided and protected those of us who are older than fifty have eroded until there remain only vestiges of restraint — about as effective as a lion's cage with paper bars! Our society used to be characterized by Judeo-Christian morals, so that even a non-believer felt checked and guided by their presence. Since the Second World War, we have seen everything devolve, more and more rapidly.

Movies that would have been banned in the fifties are now rated PG. We have stood by as curse words and nudity have become commonplace. Now, explicit intercourse is not even X-rated, much less banned.

Novels describing explicit intercourse used to be banned. Today, most novelists think if they don't include vivid descriptions of sexual activity, their works have no chance of selling — and they may be right! And so it goes in every field — magazines, short stories, TV shows, fashions, strip joints, acceptance of office love-affairs, stag parties which turn into orgies, wife-swapping, to say nothing of shady tactics in industry and corruption at all levels of government — all of which encourages young people to think they can get away with anything!

Today's society has become decidedly anti-Christ. No Christian family can assume that their neighborhood and community will help them raise their children morally. We must recognize that our society will work to destroy everything we stand for as Christians. If our children are to be escorted safely through the jungle of immorality we inhabit today, there can be no substitute for vigilance and consecrated, determined teaching and modeling of Christian virtues.

This does not mean that we should become "uptight" and lock our children into a parental police state. That would be the quickest way to create rebellion and ensure immorality. Rather, our own lives as parents must be kept sexually impeccable. "Penthouse" and "Playboy" have no place whatsoever in a Christian home. X-rated movies are always off-limits, to adults as well as children. R-rated films should be allowed for pre-teens only infrequently, and then as grounds for teaching, lest our children become young adults too naive to stand, unequipped to handle the world's shocks and sinfulness.

Church attendance must be consistent and confined to churches which believe God means what His Word says. Those who raise children in churches which give only lip-service to the Lord and regard His laws as irrelevant for today, need not bemoan that they did all they could for their children, when trouble besets them! Those who raise children in homes and churches which teach only religious legalism most often drive young people into rebellion. Those who communicate by the quality of their lives a joyful and meaningful relationship with a living Lord who dwells in us and walks with us, holding us accountable while loving us unconditionally, prepare the young to stand morally in the midst of our perverse generation.

Above all, parents need to give warm human affection to their children. Real love wards off the false. Honest affection insulates young people from the need for inappropriate touching. It leaves no vacuums to be filled by lust.

Nurture and parental communication gird young people with wisdom. "Communication" means grace-filled, one-on-one interchanges, not stony-faced Papas handing down the "law" to sniveling teens. Nurture means *time* spent *with*. Two quotes from Marshall Hamilton's book, *Father's Influence on Children*, (Nelson Hall, Chicago, 1977) convey this point:

> Father influence has been a factor commonly included in studies of the causes of juvenile delinquency. In his study of 44,448 cases in Philadelphia, Monahan (1957) notes, "For white boys the percentage of all cases in the recidivist class increases from 32 where both parents are married and living together to 38 where the father is dead and the boy is with his mother, to 42 where both parents are dead and the child is with a surrogate family, to 46 where the parents are living apart and the child is with the mother, to 49 where the parents are divorced, to 55 where the boy is living with his unmarried mother" (p. 257). He noted similar patterns for white girls,

and for black children of both sexes. (Page 22)

Hoffman (1971) looked at the effects of father-absence on conscience development in 497 seventh-grade white children; ... The father-absent boys had lower scores on maximum guilt, internal moral judgment, acceptance of blame, moral values, conformity to rules, and higher scores on overt aggression. There were no significant differences for girls. Hoffman reasoned that it was the absence of a paternal model that led to the detrimental effect of father-absence. (Page 27)

The best human antidote to societal influence has always been and will always be parents who take the time to be *with* their children, and who model Christian teaching.

Personal Causes for Fornication

The foremost personal cause for fornication is parental failure. Jean Piaget, a French moral sociologist, propounded a law we have found to be absolutely true: "If a young person keeps himself (or herself) pure, he (or she) loves and respects father and/or mother." The inverse is equally valid: "If a young person commits fornication, he (or she) hates or disrespects father and/or mother."

(I am not addressing general societal dysfunctions here, but the common individual failures of many parents. Nor do I mean to indicate that those parents are totally to blame; young people as well as adults must bear the responsibility for their own choices.)

Every girl growing up "knows" she is a gift of God to ravish her daddy's heart. If he gives her affectionate attention and communicates often with her, later on she will know her worth as a woman. She discovers what it is to be feminine by experiencing the man-woman relationship in the "safe place" of her father's heart. His attentions build wholesome "lodging places" for her husband later.

I have counseled women who have won beauty contests. But when I asked them if they were beautiful, the immediate response was, "No!" On the other hand, some women who were actually unattractive said without hesitation, "Yes, I believe I'm beautiful!" The difference lay in whether or not their fathers had complimented and affirmed them.

If the father is inattentive, or abusive (physically or emotionally), he cripples her ability to know herself as a worthwhile person. If he denigrates or molests her, her self-esteem is shattered. Girls who can't resist sexual advances almost always have had fathers who at best did not know how to nurture them, or at worst did what destroyed their ability to value and protect their chastity. In most who have fallen, counseling reveals strong needs to punish their fathers or to throw their glory away.

If a girl does not receive enough affectionate touches and affirmations, a great hole grows in her heart, needing to be filled. Later, when a young man begins to touch and hold her, she may find herself not wanting him to stop. She may not desire sexual intercourse at all. What she wants is to be cherished, to feel chosen and valued. But she may not know that most young men can't hold a girl without becoming excited to the point where they press for more and more. Before long, he becomes too aroused and insistent. She may not have the moral or physical strength to deny him.

Once she has given herself away, several things can drag even a determined Christian girl into promiscuity: First, her glory and self-esteem are despoiled, so she may think, "Why shouldn't I get whatever I can out of boys and sex?" Second, she has been awakened and aroused sexually. Her body and heart have discovered what God meant to be the apex of intimacy (but only within the confines of marriage) and even though her conscience warns her, she is now drawn as never before by the power of the sex drive.

Third, her reputation soon precedes her. The male

grapevine usually has ready data on who is "easy." Fourth, her resolve in Christ ebbs away. Disgust, shame, fear of disease and pregnancy, or Christian conscience may shore her up from time to time, but each time she lets down, she slides closer to, "Oh, what's the use, I might as well." Eventually, she may simply give up and let herself go completely.

Some young Christian women, by the grace of God, repent and turn themselves around. Disgust and shame may finally strengthen resolve beyond assault, or love for the Lord may revive and chastise the heart so sorely that she will not let herself go again. But though she may have become a compassionate and humble servant of the Lord, the price was never worth it. Her joy at being something special and unique for only one man is gone forever. *Virginity can only be given once; it can never be regained.* Love can never again have the freshness, the delight, and the glory of mutual discovery meant to be reserved for the honeymoon alone.

Girls know their womanhood by their mother's example as well. If a mother is someone worthy of emulation, her daughter is twice blessed: first, she is confirmed in the rightness of becoming the feminine person she was created to be; second, she has a role model to follow which invites and encourages her womanhood. Her femininity then becomes sacred, something worthy of protecting.

I have spoken with many Christian young women who fell to promiscuity, or frigidity, in reaction to what they saw their mothers becoming, and the attendant feelings of revulsion. Promiscuity comes from exactly the same root as frigidity — inability to enter into true intimacy and corporateness. Both promiscuity and frigidity arise in women in that they can't be vulnerable — because they can't believe anyone could see and cherish who and what they really are. In actual fact, a woman is a lovely breath of God expressed through a desirable body and personality. But she thinks she is a mess, because her mother's example taught her that lie.

Promiscuity never prepares a girl to become a better lover for her husband! It always disequips. I have counseled hundreds of young people who had bought Satan's lie that premarital sexual experience would prepare them to be better lovers when married. Intercourse before marriage, with others or with intended spouses, always results in a damaged capacity to cherish one another in holiness! Routinely, when couples come to me because of an inability to enjoy marital sex, I check to see whether one or both have been promiscuous. Almost always, I find that has been the case.

Most of the feminists Paula and I have known are shackled at their core by an incapability to accept who they are as women. They project their inner wars into outer crusades to champion women's rights. (However, some women are wholesomely and rightly concerned to advance the cause of women, as much for men's sake as for their own.)

A boy first learns what it is to be a man by relating to his father. The word "gentleman" means to me "*gentle*-man, my father, George." I never heard my father speak one word of disrespect toward or about my mother. I never heard him curse or raise his voice at her. I was ten before I knew my mother had any other name than Mom or "Sweetheart." I saw him give her affection and great respect at all times. His example wrote on my heart, "That's what I want to be." It told me what it is to be a man. I grew up wanting to respect and cherish what a woman is because my father showed me the nature of a man.

He was, moreover, faithful to my mother and to the marriage vows. I never heard foul sexual jokes from him or found any form of pornography in his possessions. And my brother and I knew that if we voiced the slightest word or tone of disrespect towards our mother, we had a "tiger" on our hands! We were never allowed to sass her or to act in any way other than utter respect. If we did, his temper was instant-on — and rightly so. My children have been raised in the same way.

My mother carefully taught me, "Jackie (she called me), no man ever curses in front of a woman. No man is a man at all who ever strikes a lady. A man treats his wife with respect, as a lady, at all times." That teaching could find lodging places in me because my parents modeled it. All of this means that there are boundaries in me I cannot pass. Respect of the personhood of women is built-in. I can't claim any credit for it. I can only praise and thank God for the parents He gave me.

My mother had failings. Her critical tongue was like a dagger which many times left me emotionally bleeding. When that happens to boys, they can develop a need to defile women. Resentment toward mothers is one of the greatest reasons young men commit fornication. But my parents' example built a hedge about me that my resentments could not tear down.

A boy learns secondarily what it is to be a man by relating to his mother. If her example is good, he gains respect for all women and wants to relate righteously to them. If her hands are soothing in times of hurt, her words reassuring and upbuilding, her heart a safe lodging place for low or exalted feelings (Prov. 31:11-12), his heart learns to trust as it should in the care of a wife. He understands his role as man toward woman by observing the place his mother gives to his father. If she gives him honor and esteem, evoking nobility, her son will desire to be a protector and provider who wants to lay down his life for his wife's good.

If, on the other hand, he sees his mother emotionally castrating his father, something in him recoils. He learns to close himself in and to attack before he can be attacked. If she demolishes with her tongue, showing disrespect and disapproval of his father, he resents her whether or not he is aware of his feelings. His bitter-root judgment expects the woman of his life to treat him as he saw his mother wounding his father, and he prepares his defenses in advance so as to have a wife but not be united to her heart. He cannot bond in intimacy.

Disrespect of women thus makes him unable to

honor the sacrosanct nature of women's sexuality. Women become "playthings," objects to be used and cast aside. "Penthouse" and "Playboy" (and other porno magazines) appeal to men who remain boys at heart, incapable of the corporateness and intimacy of true marriage. Deeply abiding respect should quench inappropriate fires of sexual desire in young or old men. But men raised by mothers who dishonor develop a need to punish, use and corrupt women. They look for momentary titillations of the flesh rather than mutual respect and satisfaction over the years.

Christian teenagers who have had good, affectionate parenting have been equipped to withstand today's societal pressures. Normally, such teenagers will remain virginal. If they do fall, it is most often because of overwhelming circumstances. But teenagers who have suffered poor upbringing have been disequipped and disarmed. Unless the grace of God intervenes, they will lose their virginity, and probably will become promiscuous.

When temptations beset us, the decisive factor is what has been lodged in the heart from childhood (Prov. 22:6)

The second major personal cause for fornication among Christians is "going steady." Going steady in itself is alright. It is the most common prelude to marriage proposals. But many young people fail to comprehend the dynamic increase of sexual power as relationships deepen. Sharing is the springboard for intimacy. As togetherness grows, and shared experiences open our hearts more and more to one another, our bodies naturally expect to participate in that oneness. Feelings of tenderness seek to be expressed in sexual touches.

When I was a boy, we had favorite swimming holes in the rivers of southern Kansas. But we soon learned we could never leap into the same river twice. Where the river had been deep might now be shallow, and vice versa. Relationships are like that. One never knows when the heart may crack open and let down the barriers of sexual resistance. A young man may think he has measured himself and his lover well — and thus he remains safe and proper for many days. But the very next day sexual passions may rise beyond what has been that "safe" level, and he may find himself suddenly incapable of controlling his emotions or his actions.

How perverse it is that pitfalls happen most often just when the couple think they are safe! After a fight, for example, he might figure she surely wouldn't want anything to do with him. Whereas in fact pain and the prospect of loneliness may have finally convinced her heart, "This is the one I can't stand to lose." Her desire to keep him may overcome her wisdom and restraint. Or, after a time of separation, they might think they will have to rebuild slowly and couldn't possibly be overwhelmed as yet by desire. But the old saw is true that "Absence makes the heart grow fonder." Or, when agreement to abstain from passion has been a hard-won mutual decision, they relax and think to trust one another. But they may be unaware that their very struggle for mutuality has opened their hearts to each other so deeply that their passions are poised to find satisfaction sexually.

The third major personal cause of fornication among Christians is fear of rejection. Countless young women over the years have confessed to us, "I didn't want to, but I was afraid he'd leave me." Somehow they have swallowed the lie that giving themselves sexually will cement the relationship. After the wedding, lovingly yielding to each other will weld hearts together. Before marriage, it disappoints the spirit of a man, even though he may think he is delighted. Respect has been tarnished.

Sex after marriage increases holy respect for the other. Beforehand, it can demolish. Many young men who were on the brink of proposing felt cheated by the premature "gift," and some have deserted the relationship. If the alliance does go ahead, the couple begin wedded life with unhealed hurts in their hearts and unanswered questions in their heads. She may harbor feelings of being unfairly taken and thus cheapened. Both may retain fear that the other may not be able to stand against temptation. The ability to trust fully may thus be irretrievably crushed. (It must be remembered that we are speaking of well-intentioned Christians. Non-Christians may be so dead in conscience as to find all of this irrelevant.)

The fourth major personal cause for fornication among unwary Christians is the sudden message from the heart and spirit, "This is the one." In the spring of my junior year in college when Paula and I had been going steady for about six months, my parents had to declare bankruptcy. I announced at table in the Commons one day that it appeared I would not be able to return for my final year. Paula knew by the pain in her heart that I was "the one," and immediately her defenses were gone. Everything inside said, "Go ahead, it's alright." Her conscience simply shut down. Where we had easily controlled ourselves before, now it was all we could do to stop.

A fifth reason accompanies the fourth — long engagements. Our son Tim met Victoria at the end of his third year in high school. That fall, they knew they were meant for each other. By the spring of his senior and her junior year, they were engaged. All during his freshman year in college, he drove home each weekend to be with Victoria. Tim had more wisdom and restraint than I could have mustered; he knew that Victoria should have a year of college away from home without being married. So they waited. Their engagement lasted two-and-a-half years, normal for our grandparents' generation but impossibly long for today's.

Recently, they told us what a struggle it had been. They took refuge in group activities. Since their university allowed men and women in each other's rooms at any hour of the day or night, they always left the door wide open. Other students would pass by and "helpfully" shut the door, thinking they wanted privacy. Doggedly, they would reopen it. Although Victoria had a TV in her room, they went to the lounge to watch TV, out in the open. Nevertheless, they told us it was all they could do to make it to their wedding as virgins, even with Christian determination and much prayer. They said, "We would never advise couples today to have long engagements."

Part of the problem with long engagements is that having denied themselves for so long a time, when it becomes okay, sometimes the couple can't easily reverse themselves and enjoy one another. Too many "no" messages have been sent into the "control room." Reprograming may take awhile.

How To Prevent Fornication

First, get involved in Christian youth groups. But be circumspect in choosing a group — sadly, some have become quite carnal. Our son Mark, hoping to find moral Christian fellowship while he was in seminary, attended a singles' group in a nearby church. He was shocked and offended to find those young people loudly praising God on the weekends while most of them were fornicating mightily all week! We hope that is the exception rather than the rule. Young couples especially should be encouraged to seek wholesome group activities which allow neither solitude nor time for temptation.

Second, spend time with one or both families, especially the parents. This not only affords ready-made chaperones, it builds respectful relationships which serve as checks on passions.

Third, spend limited time together. Wise couples limit themselves to one or two dates a week. They deny desires to be together every minute of the day and night. "Familiarity breeds contempt" — contempt for the sacredness of sex and the body.

Fourth, read the Scriptures and pray together. Inviting the Lord as guest on the couch does wonders toward squelching passions!

Fifth, avoid potentially compromising or tempting situations. Paula and I have been appalled to hear of Christian young people blithely planning to spend weekends alone together at a friend's cabin! Even separate motel rooms on long trips have a tendency to meld into one. For Christian couples trying to maintain morality, privacy is a most dangerous companion.

Sixth, stay away from parties where it is known that alcohol or drugs will be present. Couples who refrain from alcohol and drugs need to be aware that empathetic defilement from others less upright can invade and disarm good judgment. And some people delight to see moral couples fall into sin. Some are not above slipping alcohol or drugs into seemingly harmless food and drink. We know of an upright young man who went berserk when someone slipped LSD into his soft drink, and of a young virgin who became the willing victim of a "gang bang" when affected by a seemingly innocent drink.

Seventh, worship in church and serve Christ in ministry together. However, Christians should beware. Sharing deeply in mutual labor builds relationships which want to express love more fervently. Many have been surprised to find sexual passions rising immediately following a great worshipful time with the Lord. Ours is an incarnational faith. There is no way we can separate the parts of our being so as to be excited spiritually but not emotionally and physically.

Many Christians have thought themselves safe from temptation because they were experiencing a spiritual high. They thought, "Surely Satan can't come to tempt me when I am so full of the Spirit." But Satan came to test our Lord Jesus *during* His forty-day fast, when He was surely most close to God (Matt. 4:1-11). Being spiritual does not protect us; it heightens our emotions and senses so that we are more vulnerable to sexual and other temptations than at any other time! Many of the Lord's mighty men have fallen because they did not understand this simple fact of our creation. The holiness of serving and the hours spent laboring for others may indeed strengthen our resolve to stand morally. But we must not thereby relax our vigilance and think that we have been made safe by being in our Lord's presence.

Though earlier I said that being in the Lord's presence would help to get rid of defilement, and that remains true, being in His presence does not void temptation. Defilement comes upon us from outside; but temptation arises from within. Spiritual highs turn us on, so that all manner of passions can be set free.

How To Heal When Fornication Has Happened

Confession is always in order, and the sooner the better. Clergymen and priests are obviously the first and best ones in whose presence one should make confessions. But a young person can be greatly helped by any mature and knowledgeable Christian. (Roman Catholics or members of episcopal and sacramental denominations should remember that their church normally requires confession be made to the proper authorities.)

The one who confesses should look for the following helps and, if they are not forthcoming, should continue to seek help until they are:

One — the confessor who hears the confession must know his authority to forgive sins, and express it forthrightly (John 20:23 & James 5:16).

Two — the confessor must know to probe for whatever roots caused the fornication. If the confessor does not enable the growth of forgiveness in the penitent one for his father (or for whomever may have caused the root to grow), and bring about reconciliation, the person is likely to fornicate again (Matt.3:10 & Heb. 12:15).

Three — the confessor who hears the confession must know to separate the spirits of those who have cohabited (1 Cor. 6:15-16 & Heb. 4:12).

Four — the confessor who hears the confession should know to pray deeply cleansing prayers, until the person feels free and whole again — making the penitent a worthy gift to a spouse later on (1 Cor. 6:11 & 2 Cor. 5:17). Self-esteem must be restored.

Five — Instruction in the Word of God concerning the holiness of sex should be followed by admonitions not to sin again (1 Cor. 6:8-20 & John 8:3-11).

Six — some counsel and instruction should be given concerning the other person who was involved in the fornication. If the two parties to the sin are allowed to resume their former relationship, the chances are that fornication will happen again. They should remain apart, or some strong safeguards must be built into the relationship until time creates distance or marriage permits copulation.

Seven — if the fornication has become known, reconciliation with and acceptance by the parents and other family members (or whomever else has become involved) should be attempted. Wisdom dictates that discretion should guard the lips of all. If parents are *not* aware, divulging the sin could be more wounding than helpful. Perhaps friends do not need to know. Healing needs to be sought wherever there are known fractures and woundings. But dying embers need not be stirred unnecessarily.

Some, who committed fornication and subsequently asked for and received forgiveness have asked us whether they should reveal their past to their fiance(e)s. We believe that honesty is the best policy. It is never good to begin a marriage withholding secrets. If either cannot stand to know the whole truth about the other, the relationship is not capable of withstanding the pressures of marriage and should not be allowed to proceed further. However, wise lovers will be sensitive about where, how and when to share how much. Pray that the Lord will provide the best opportunity.

Sensitive honesty does not fracture trust; it establishes it. Lies and secrets become like land-mines waiting to be stepped on. Better to own up to shortcomings and failures now than to be hurt by revelations later.

Our spirits sense unspoken things. Deception causes our spirits to nag at our minds that something's wrong, and that makes relationships edgy and tense. Together let's invite the Lord to heal all the past. Let's start life together clean and free.

Finally, parents can destroy young people whose sins have become known. A parent who yells "You slut!" forfeits his God-given right to comfort and restore. Condemnation has no place in Christ (Rom. 8:1). Forgiveness needs to be accompanied by compassion, repeated expressions of acceptance, and the parents' own repentance that their failings (and there usually have been some) jeopardized their child.

If pregnancy is involved, abortion should not even be thought of. The young woman needs to be assured that she still belongs to the family, and so does the child within her. It is not wise to *force* a daughter to relinquish her child to adoption. Careful discussions should pave the way for prayerful decisions which fully respect both her and the father's wishes and the desires of the prospective grandparents. Whenever possible, the child should be kept within the family, at best with the mother. If she is too young or, for any other reason, needs help taking care of her baby, the grandparents or a relative can keep the child until the mother is able to assume her parental duties. Arrangements can and should be made, with this key in mind at all times: we are called by God to provide the very best we can for the life of that unborn child, *within the family.* That responsibility has first priority in any and all deliberations.

Although they are very serious matters, loss of virginity and consequent pregnancy are not the end of the world and should not be treated as such. The Body of Christ is called to be a healing body of love. A young woman in our church conceived a child out of wedlock. Our son, Loren, who was the pastor, said to the congregation at the time for dedication, "You all know the circumstances of this child's birth. We don't know how long it will be before this child has a daddy. If there is any man in this congregation who would come forward to stand beside the mother and share her vows to raise the boy in a Christian way, let him come forward."

Every man in the congregation arose as one and came to stand and take those vows! Some could do no more than that. Others picked him up after Sunday school and complimented him on his efforts. Some took him to picnics and ball games. Four years later, one of the men who had stood that day fell in love with the mother and married her. Today, that boy, who had one hundred stand-in fathers, has one real stepfather who loves him, and his mother has never known condemnation nor rejection. She knows herself to be a valued, loved and honored member of a church which stood by her in her time of need.

5
Pornography, Voyeurism, Fantasy and Masturbation

Definitions

I define *pornography* as the viewing of prurient materials such as photographs, magazines and novels, and "adult" (actually childish) X-rated movies. I define *voyeurism* as compulsive peeping or watching living persons undress, maneuver nakedly, or engage in sexual activity. Pornography is thus the viewing of inanimate objects which portray bodies and sex lustfully, while voyeurism is the lustful viewing of living persons.

Pornography and voyeurism sometimes lead into fornication, adultery and rape, but that is not the subject I address here. The question is: *"Why do Christians fall into these sins?"* The problem is not merely why some Christians become involved in pornography, voyeurism, fantasy and masturbation, but why they become blindly addicted and compulsive about these activities. The Church today wonders how and why so many well-intentioned Christians could have become enmeshed in these traps of the flesh as have scandalized the faith in these times.

From the moment Adam and Eve knew they were naked and sewed fig leaves to cover themselves (Gen. 3:7), all mankind has been bedeviled by sexual impulses. It is normal to have them; it is abnormal not to. "Normal" does not mean "okay," only "common to all." Most little boys and girls play "doctor and nurse" at one time or another. Even before the teenage years, when the hormones turn on and the "brains fall out," children may play with their genital organs and stimulate themselves.

Most teenage boys, and some girls, get hold of porno magazines and feel deliciously sinful while giggling through them. Such things, common to most childhoods, are not yet addictive or compulsive. Teen-agers soon pass through them to maturity. Born-anew Christians learn by prayer to overcome "the lust of the eyes" and check improper sexual impulses. Their sinful childhood experiences and subsequent repentances serve to arm their minds with warning signals and the wisdom to refrain. We need not fear the common sinful dabblings of childhood; it is not these which create or cause addictions and compulsions.

Our question is why some Christians fail to pass through, why they can't learn as others do from such experiences and then leave them alone. Why, in some, sexual fascination becomes so addictive and compulsive that, for instance, TV evangelists of international stature could jeopardize world-wide, multi-million-dollar ministries and, more importantly, the reputation of the Body of Christ for the sake of a few hours of sin! People wonder how anything could become that blindingly addictive.

> For while we were in the flesh, the sinful passions, which were aroused by the Law, were at work in the members of our body to bear fruit for death. (Rom. 7:5)

> But sin, taking opportunity through the commandment, produced in me coveting of every kind; for apart from the Law sin is dead. And I was once alive apart from the Law; but when the commandment came, sin became alive, and I died; and this commandment, which was to result in life, proved to result in death for me; for sin, taking opportunity through the commandment, deceived me, and through it killed me. (VV. 8-11)

The laws of God are holy and good. Their purpose, however, is *not* to enable us to do good, but to convict us of sin (Rom. 3:19-20). Only the grace of our Lord Jesus Christ keeps us from sin.

But these Scriptures indicate that the Law causes us to sin! How?

All of us were born with unholy desires. They come as part of the package of being human in the likeness of Adam and Eve. "Folly is bound up in the heart of a child, but the rod of discipline will drive it far from him" (Prov. 22:15, NIV). Given the sinful nature we all inherit, when "no-no's" are placed in front of us (and they must be), two unhealthy things can happen: one, rebellion arises, tempting and driving us to do the very thing the Law says not to! Christians normally easily handle such rebellious desires by prayer. For many Christians, walking in freedom is nearly automatic.

Two, a dynamic of suppression and expression sets in. Full treatment of this subject can be found in our book, *Restoring the Christian Family*, Chapter 16, entitled "Death Under the Law, but Life in the Spirit." (I suggest that readers would profit best by studying that chapter before reading further. Much of what I say here may be missed or misunderstood without adequate comprehension of the dynamic of suppression and expression). Suffice it to say that when we try to be righteous, not by grace but by our own efforts, we must suppress nasty impulses.

If, for example, an improper sexual impulse arises, and we don't know how to release it in prayer to the Lord, then we must deny expression to that urge. We push it down and refuse to act on it. That in no way ends its activity; it only redirects it. Denied healthy expression, impulses will vent in perverted ways. And more suppression only multiplies the need to express! Like holding a tennis ball under water: the further one pushes it down, the more power it gains to shoot up and out! Once a Christian swallows the lie that he must win the battle (in his flesh) — the moment he can't by restful prayer let the Lord crucify his wrong desires — he falls into an

ever-accelerating dynamic of inner warfare. In proportion
to his determination to obey the Law, to that degree the
Law and his sinful nature combine to drive him into
unmanageable compulsions. For this reason, religious
people fall to gross sexual sins!

That is what Paul meant when he said what I quoted
above. Let's see it again, this time observing the emphases:

> But sin, taking opportunity through the
> commandment, produced in me coveting of
> every kind; for apart from the Law sin is dead.
> And I was once alive apart from the Law; but
> when the commandment came, sin became
> alive, and I died; and this commandment, which
> was to result in life, proved to result in death for
> me; for sin, taking opportunity through the
> commandment, deceived me, and through it
> killed me. (Rom. 7:8-11)

In effect, Adam and Eve had said to God, "We're not
going to let You raise us. We'll do it ourselves." Our wise
Father knew that if mankind would just try to live up to
His commandments (necessarily in the flesh because the
Holy Spirit had not yet come), we would discover we
can't. That way, we would realize our desperate need for
a Savior.

He knew that every time we decided not to act on
an impulse in a way forbidden by the Law, we would have
no recourse but to deny that urge expression. That
suppression would create ever stronger needs to express:

> So I find it to be a law that when I want to
> do right, evil lies close at hand. For I delight in
> the law of God, in my inmost self, but I see in
> my members another law at war with the law
> of my mind and making me captive to the law
> of sin which dwells in my members. (Rom.
> 7:21-23, RSV)

The Lord knew the more determinedly we would try in the flesh to live His commandments, the sooner we would reap the impossibility of it without Him. He gave us the Law so that *through* it we might be brought to the death of ourselves on His cross.

The tragedy is that so many Christians keep trying to live like Christ without letting His indwelling Spirit do it for them. Consequently, the more Christians strive religiously under the Law, the sooner and more grossly they can explode into sins! Christians who really want to love and serve the Lord righteously have wound up doing the most outrageous things imaginable: Paula and I have ministered to women who have been to well-known "Christian" counselors who, upon learning that their clients had suppressed childhood molestations, induced them to undress before them, and then proceed to molest them again! This was supposed to help them recall what happened and somehow relieve them of the pressure of it!

We came to a town in which an internationally known evangelist had seduced a young girl and gotten her pregnant, and then would not admit that he even knew her. We were called upon to minister to her parents, trying to explain how such a thing could happen.

A pastor we knew of could hardly wait to slip into an out-of-the-way, home-video store so he could stock up on X-rated movies (whenever his wife was out of town). Another pastor found himself periodically binging on fantasizing while he masturbated (though his wife was a fully sufficient lover). It may be hard to believe that the Christians in these examples actually wanted to live righteously, but they did. When Christians do not understand the dynamics of suppression and expression, they can be driven by inner factors to do things they never would have thought possible. Pressures can mount until common sense and discernment are destroyed and the laws of God are forgotten or rationalized away.

Another "Christian" counselor, whenever he learned that a woman considered herself to be frigid, made it his most common "therapy" to get into bed with her and make love to her until she was fully aroused — and then send her home to her husband quickly so she could make love to him before she had time to cool down! One woman's counselor not only regularly seduced her, but after a while he brought in another man so the counselor could watch while this man had intercourse with her! And on it goes — and I have not even deemed it appropriate to reveal some of the more gross things that have been confessed to us by victims of "Christian" leaders (see Eph. 5:12).

Whenever Christians fall into fleshly, religious striving after righteousness, they set themselves into a terrible dynamic which may explode into unimaginable expressions of sin. Once a particular form of sexual sinning becomes identified as the way to find satisfaction for inner driving forces, since that sin rather creates more hunger than it satisfies, both the frequency of need and the grossness required to "satisfy" it inevitably increase. I say "may explode" because not all do. Sometimes grace intervenes to cool the passions, or the perpetrator recognizes and stops Satan's game of delusion, or revulsion produces such godly grief that he comes to real repentance (2 Cor. 7:9,10). Sadly, however, far too many men and women who were determined to live righteously for Christ find themselves trapped by their striving, into the very sins they detested.

Some widely known televangelists of our day have fallen that way, grievously wounding the Body of Christ. These men need our forgiveness and our prayers. We need to understand the forces that drove them, and other Christian leaders, if we are to pray appropriately.

The question is, why do the prayers of such men and women fail? Why are they unable to find easy release from sexual drives through talking it out with God? What causes them (and so many times some of us as well) to fall back under the Law? The rule is that where major malformed roots in childhood have been healed, Christians can normally take improper desires and impulses restfully to the cross. All of us are occasionally subject to sinful impulses. We can usually easily "reckon" such things as dead (Rom. 6:11). But the corollary rule is that whenever unhealed roots of sufficient corruption lie beneath the surface, perfunctory normal prayers and reckoning cannot successfully bring sinful sexual urges to death on the cross.

Unhealed factors in the heart continually and insistently resurrect sinful passions and practices, which then demand expression. So the Christian prays harder, trying to control his mysteriously mounting sexual urges. But that is like trying during a rainstorm to dry up a river with a teaspoon! His prayers won't stop his passions.

The battle seems to be all his own, without the help of the Holy Spirit. Satan takes advantage and adds to his struggle. Increasingly frequent failures and consequent stresses then throw him into a frenzy of fleshly striving to control himself. Grace is there, but to him it's gone. He is now caught in a dynamic of ever-accelerating suppression and expression under the Law — into eventual explosion!

Countless Christians have fallen into that trap. Historically, when Americans began the great westward movement of the nineteenth century, the Holy Spirit had to devise a way of reaching a fast-moving populace. The answer was evangelism in "sawdust and tears" revivals. Preachers reduced the gospel to the simplest, most essential matters for conversion — "Hit them with a just and angry God and drive them into the arms of a loving Jesus" — preach guilt and repentance and bring them to the altar to receive forgiveness and the new birth. There is nothing wrong with that. By it the Lord converted a nation! Revival preaching is needed all the more as our nation falls further into sin in an anti-christ culture.

But that "reduced gospel" was not intended to tell the whole story, and it could not. It said little or nothing about the continuing struggle to sanctify the heart. In the sixteenth century, Ignatius Loyola founded the Jesuit order, which ignited and largely carried the greatest missionary effort ever in the history of Christianity. Loyola taught and applied tough disciplines for sanctification after conversion, saying of St. Francis Xavier, for example, "The lumpiest lump of dough I ever kneaded."

Benedictines also established and followed a "rule of life" for sanctification after conversion. (Some Protestants need to beware of making judgments here. Read about these men. You'll find they were truly born anew!) John Wesley founded the Methodist Church, so named because its adherents insisted upon a "method" of sanctification after conversion. Wesley's followers were among the leaders of the Great Awakening in America during the eighteenth century. All these men of God knew the fulness of the gospel. They knew the need to bring continuing roots of sinfulness to death on the cross long after we receive Jesus as Lord and Savior.

But during the second great awakening in America, during the nineteenth century, generations of Christians received nothing but the "reduced gospel." Sunday after Sunday, they heard only evangelism preached. Many men responded to the call of God, picked up their Bibles and went out to preach — without benefit of education. We intend no judgment here; the Lord needed and called them. But most knew little or nothing beyond the "reduced Gospel"! They did not know the Church's accumulated knowledge and wisdom for dealing with the pesky practices of the old nature after conversion.

Thinking they were totally new creatures and their born-anew parishioners ought likewise to be able to walk rightly in Christ, they laid on heavy exhortations: "You are new creatures, now live up to it! Do it! Just try harder!" Though their members were positionally new creatures, they continued to be plagued by unholy passions which kept springing up from undead roots! They could *not* do it.

Exhortation only threw them into fleshly striving. Then, in their determination to be holy, many fell into the dynamic described above, until cycles of suppression and expression either forced them into sin or drove them into lives of quiet despair. (Some, wiser and humbler, broke free from the cycle and found true peace in Christ, but

I wish the reader could sit in my office and listen to the defeated, confused life-stories I hear, all because so many Christians have not heard the gospel of sanctification following conversion!)

Many experienced what we call the "teeter-totter effect." On Sunday, they celebrated their new creation in Christ, singing songs of thankfulness that the old man was dead and the new had been born. By Wednesday, many were wallowing in defeat, as roots which had sprung up impelled them into sin — child-beating, pornography, voyeurism, molestation, incest, lying, cheating, stealing, whatever. Some did not fall but had to battle incessantly, wondering where the joy and ease of heart they first knew in Christ had gone. On Thursday, many were sinking into depression.

The next Sunday required a "higher high" to feel good again. And so it went, each week's struggles and defeats demanding more ecstatic release the next Sunday, until some Christians either gave up trying to live the Christian life and fell back to sin altogether or quit coming to church because they felt like hypocrites. For all too many, eventually the actual living of life had nothing to do with what they celebrated. Christianity had become a religious thing to be done on Sunday, but nobody except the naive idealists should expect to *live* it!

On a recent TV talk show, several men and women who regularly and openly commit adultery as a life-style spoke of themselves as ". . .good Christians who love Jesus and attend church every Sunday!" These were born-anew people, some of whom claimed to have the Holy Spirit! But they saw no contradiction between what they were doing and their profession of faith in Christ! Not knowing how to conquer bitter roots that cause sins (Heb. 12:15), convinced by inadequate theologies that they weren't supposed to, they had fallen so often they had concluded faith has nothing to do with how they actually live life!

Historically, during the Second Great Awakening, many evangelists began to elevate the conversion experience beyond what Scripture claims for it.

Conversion does have tremendous impact: it changes our direction from hell to heaven. It washes all our sins away in the blood of Christ. It deals our sin nature a death blow. It effects many immediate, dramatic changes in our personality and character (which, sadly, helps to convince us that we are totally and forever different). It imbues us with the Holy Spirit and renews our own spirit. It restores us to sonship and grants us access to the heart of God through prayer. It changes the angel guard from Satan's to the Lord's (Heb. 1:14, Ps. 91:11). It makes us new creatures in Christ (2 Cor. 5:17). But it does not end the process of sanctification and transformation; it begins it! (See the first seven chapters of our book, *The Transformation of the Inner Man.*)

When we are born anew, it becomes our task to respond to the Holy Spirit as He daily calls us to die to whatever roots and practices continue resisting the impact of the blood and the cross. After His disciples had been with Him awhile, Jesus asked, "And why do you call Me, 'Lord, Lord,' and do not do what I say?" (Luke 6:46). He answered His own question by teaching them that they must "dig deep" (vs. 48) to their "foundations" to make sure those foundations had been built on the rock of His character. If they did not, they would not be able to stand in times of trial (the rush of great waters). The command to us is to dig deep *after* conversion.

Preachers and teachers soon began to elevate the conversion experience as though it did everything once for all. "Come down here to this altar, and you'll be a totally new creature forever!" In one respect, that call is true. The tragedy is that it omits the daily work thereafter of crucifying the flesh.

> Brethren, my heart's desire and my prayer to God for them is for their salvation. For I bear them witness that they have a zeal for God, but not in accordance with knowledge. For not knowing about God's righteousness, and seeking to establish their own, they did not subject

themselves to the righteousness of God. For Christ is the end of the law for righteousness to everyone who believes. (Rom. 10:1-4)

A cruel irony is that many Christians who have used that Scripture to convert unbelievers have failed to see that it applies equally to born-anew Christians who, without the discipline of daily crucifixion, err in thinking they are, "totally new creatures forever" and so try to live righteously by the failing strength of their own flesh! When we believe the false theology that our conversion "does it" once for all, we no longer use prayer to crucify resurrected flesh daily — and are thereby reduced to striving to live like Christ without the grace of the cross! "...for if you are living according to the flesh, you must die; but if by the Spirit you are putting to death the deeds of the body, you will live" (Rom. 8:13).

I'm sure that most of the leaders I know about who fell were convinced that their conversion experiences had made them totally new creatures. Positionally, that was true, "For by one offering He has perfected for all time those who are sanctified" (Heb 10:14), and "It is finished" (John 19:30). But St. Paul was wise enough to know that though our flesh was slain, it can come back to life, "See to it... that no root of bitterness springing up causes trouble, and by it many be defiled" (Heb. 12:15).

Many of these leaders to whom we have ministered began as quite normal people, not bothered by sexual or any other addictions. But, like most of us, their hearts contained many unhealed, fractured areas from childhood. Nevertheles, their theology told them they were totally changed men. Therefore they denied the counseling which could have helped them identify and bring to effective death the inner factors driving them into sexual trouble. Because of their inadequate theology, some fled from counseling and then denounced it as unnecessary and even harmful to born-anew Christians. Thus they were unprepared to handle the inner drives which revived under the constant pressures and stresses of intensive public ministry.

Since they thought their fractures and sins had been totally done away with once for all by their conversion, they lost sight of the admonition: "...*work out your salvation* with fear and trembling" (Phil. 2:12). They did not know how to effectively lay aside the old self with its evil practices after receiving Jesus (Col. 3:9). The true biblical way is to recognize undead flesh as it springs up, track it to its root (Matt. 3:10), and bring it fully to death by repentance, confession, forgiveness and reckoning it as dead on the cross (Gal. 2:20 & 5:24). These leaders knew about confession, repentance and forgiveness. Most of them taught it faithfully to others. But they knew little or nothing about tracking to roots nor how to crucify sinful desires anew whenever they sprang back to life. Those undead roots are thus what prevented their prayers from corralling their sinful sexual urges, and that failure threw them back into striving under the Law. They couldn't stop themselves. Their theology was incomplete. It lacked the dimension of continuing sanctification of the heart after their salvation experience.

For example: Ben was born into a religious family. When he was six, and his girl cousins were six and seven, the children played "doctor." Ben's mother found them looking at one another's private parts. Horrified, she screamed at Ben that he was a nasty little boy, and disciplined him severely. This created the idea in Ben's mind that the body is mysteriously sinful and something enticingly forbidden to play with or steal looks at. He soon found his father's porno magazines hidden in a tool chest. He "feasted" on these until his mother caught him and ranted at him some more. From then on, she kept reminding him of his sinful acts. That set up a determination in him to get back at her by whatever sneaky means he could! By his late teenage years, he was addicted to pornography, the more salacious the better.

In his early twenties, he was born anew in a dramatic experience and soon thereafter received a call to the ministry. For several years, the addiction was simply gone.

He had no desire to look at anything forbidden. In seminary, he had met and married a lovely woman who was a willing and fully satisfying sexual partner. It seemed that he was "home free." But then success, pressure and some persecution began to drain his energies. His mother had been performance-oriented, incapable of giving affection liberally without strings. Performance orientation had been built into him.

Soon he began to be plagued by vague feelings of anger and rebellion, unable to understand why he felt unloved and unappreciated when his wife was so obviously affectionate. On a whim one day, he stopped at a newsstand and bought a porno magazine. Devouring its contents somehow made him feel deliciously rebellious and mysteriously released and fulfilled (See Chapter 3, "Performance Orientation," in *The Transformation of the Inner Man*). Actually he had regressed to his earlier practice of secretly defeating his religious mother, projecting that pattern now onto "Mother Church." Before long, he was again fully addicted.

His theology told him he was a new creature. Nothing in his training had equipped him to look within himself to find and crucify bad roots. He did not know that bitter roots could "spring up" and by them many could "be defiled" (Heb. 12:15), nor that addictions like his could cause him to fulfil the next verse, ". . .that there be no immoral or godless person like Esau, who sold his own birthright for a single meal." He fought against demons of lust. Caring friends who were aware of his struggle cast away demon after demon — to no lasting avail because undealt-with roots kept inviting them back. When his addiction was discovered and he lost his pastorate, he recognized that he had indeed sold his birthright for a few forbidden "meals," but he had no inkling as to what had driven him to do it.

Repentance ran deep. Forgiveness touched his heart more fully than ever before. He became an even more successful preacher in the next church, convinced that he had "learned his lesson," sure that he was now thoroughly healed and free. But he wasn't. Causal roots had never been touched. It was not many years before he was again entrapped and overcome! The tragedy was that no one in his denomination knew how to bring such roots and habits to effective death on the cross. No one understood the inner dynamics of the heart which continually snared him in what he had now come to hate so violently. He had become a victim of undead habits and incomplete theology.

Another man to whom Paula and I ministered found himself compulsively getting into both homosexual and heterosexual affairs, as well as pornography, voyeurism and masturbation. His parents had been self-sacrificial servants of the Lord whom he admired greatly. One paradox of counseling is that it is usually easier to counsel someone who had recognizably bad parents than it is to minister to one who had saintly but imperfect parents. The reason is that resentments toward recognizably bad parents can be seen rather easily whereas loyalty blinds the eyes to the imperfections of good parents; that leaves the client mystified as to why he or she is so bad when the parents seem to be so good. It sets up a tremendous dynamic of suppressing real feelings towards the parents. And it causes hurts and angers to be projected onto others.

It took awhile for the truth to come out. Having been afraid of the dark, when he was a little boy, he would often slip into bed with his parents. Often he would arrive just as they were approaching sexual climax, and though he was now almost four years old, they would allow him to remain there while they continued into climax! Not only that, but immediately afterwards when his father would roll out and go to the bathroom, his mother would pull him on top of herself and hug him to her breasts while she was still in the throes of excitement! This continued for several more years before they finally prohibited him from their bed!

Scripture carefully warns not to arouse or excite love before the proper time (Song of Songs 2:7 & 3:5).

That series of experiences aroused all manner of

sexual urges within the boy before he had the wisdom to handle them. He had no way of knowing that such behavior was not normal. And since his parents were being so saintly, pouring their lives out in service to the Lord, he was left with no way to explain why he had such compelling sexual drives. As a boy, he was ejected from several schools, having been caught in the act of voyeurism. In his teenage years several kinds of sexual addictions took hold of him.

Then he was converted. For a while he was free. But life's stresses soon took their toll, and his sexual compulsions revived. Friends exorcised sexual demons. But since the causal roots remained untouched, they always came back worse than before.

His theology told him he ought to be a totally new creature. He set himself to believe that he was free. But that didn't work any better than casting demons away.

He spent hours and bundles of money in psychiatrists' offices. That began to help somewhat, but it remained an unsolved mystery as to where his compulsions had started and why they existed at all when his parents had seemed to be so loving and righteous in all their ways. As we talked, by the grace of the Lord and a little help from gifts of knowledge, he began to remember what his parents had allowed to happen.

For years, even after he had begun to suspect that his parents must have somehow been part of his problem, loyalty and ignorance had suppressed memories of those early unwise stimulations. Following that recollection, a stream of other foolish things in the family's life began to surface. His parents apparently had no proper concept of modesty before their children and little or no awareness of how that could affect them! His theology not only left him unequipped to handle his inner compulsions, it disequipped him by throwing him into striving to control what his theology told him was already dead.

One secular counselor I know says that whenever she is called upon to counsel a Christian, she knows she will have to deal with someone who has almost no real awareness of his true sexual feelings and, worse yet, has been taught to suppress them as unworthy or of the devil. Therefore, she says, most Christians she counsels have few or no skills for handling sexual feelings. Her judgment of course is not true for all believers, nor perhaps for most, but I would have to confess that my experiences in counseling a number of born-anew Christians too often parallel hers.

The false elevation of the conversion experience beyond what the Bible claims for it, and the consequent ignorance and neglect of the need to die daily to resurrected roots of character malformation, are among the primary reasons Christians fall to all manner of sexual sins! *And voyeurism, pornography, fantasy and masturbation seem to be especially prevalent among those believers who have gone no deeper than the truncated gospel.*

Voyeurism, pornography, fantasy and masturbation cannot grip Christians compulsively unless unhealed fractures afford opportunity. Similar woundings of personality and character lie behind all sexual sins. *No whole person falls to compulsive sexual sin.* Always some wounding, usually in childhood, has opened the door to addictive sexual trouble in adulthood. Faulty theology is a partial cause, but it alone cannot seduce Christians into addictive, compulsive behaviors. However, faulty theology can cause Christians to fail to deal properly with childhood woundings and consequent malformations of character. That gives the devil opportunity. Eventually they are plunged into addiction and destruction.

Wounds and Fractures Common to All Sexual Sinfulness and Dysfunction

1) *Lack of consistent parental nurture and discipline.*

A) Affection feeds the personal spirit with strength and builds habits of normal healthy intimacy. It constructs channels for wholesome physical touching. Such appropriate practices tend to ward off and make repulsive whatever is inappropriate. Consistent parental nurture enables a true working conscience, which acts to keep the person from sin rather than merely to convict after the event.

Lack of affection fails to build those necessary good practices in the character. It creates driving hungers which don't know where and how to find their true fulfillment. Lack of affection in childhood destroys the functioning power of the conscience (see Chapter 5, "The Slumbering Spirit," in *Healing the Wounded Spirit*).

B) Discipline builds in stopping places. It structures the heart and mind to know the law of sowing and reaping. It begets holy fear of God and respect for the persons of others. It creates the capacity to deny one's self, and desire to think first of others' welfare. It dispels the fear of self; children without discipline are afraid of their tendency to run amok, since daddy and mommy have not given them the peace and security of established limits. Discipline instills proper self-confidence (because parental discipline builds into a child the capacity to control himself, which gives him the assurance that he can handle whatever comes and make right choices).

A lack of discipline basically leaves the passions in control of the person rather than the other way around (Prov. 25:28). A lack of discipline destroys one's ability to value and respect others, and it therefore destroys one's capability to think first of others' safety and well-being. "Look out for No. 1" has thus become the by-word of the "Me-generation." The unfortunate corollary is, "If it feels good, do it!"

(It should be noted that proper discipline is administered in love, for the child's good, and though it sometimes calls for physical spanking — Prov. 13:24, 23:13 — it is never to be equated with beating, which is nothing more than violence at the expense of the child. Good discipline writes the law of sowing and reaping onto a child's heart; the pain administered is only enough to register the lesson upon the heart. Beating only inflicts pain as the parent vents his/her own emotions; it is not discipline for the child's sake in love as in Heb. 12:5-11, but against the child for the parent's sake.)

There are no more important formative factors in all of life than parental nurture and discipline (Eph. 6:4). (I cannot remember ever having counseled anyone involved in sexual sin, especially voyeurism, pornography, fantasy and masturbation, who had received sufficient affection and discipline!) Whoever would minister to the roots of sexual sins and dysfunctions must always search out and heal the childhood history in relation to affection and discipline.

2) *Lack of admirable parental teaching and modeling.*

A) Children become and do what their parents *are*, not what they *say*. Children need to see their parents model wholesome affection and respect for one another. Parents' attitudes towards sex will become their children's. Good modeling writes in: "That's what I want to be."

It's so important. Please allow me to reiterate what I said in previous chapters:

I never heard my father express a word of disrespect or insult towards my mother. I never saw him behave crossly toward her, yell at her or act out even a hint of violence. Any disrespect or back-talk we might display towards her resulted in immediate sharp discipline from him. He never touched her sexual areas in our presence, though he continually gave her hugs and quick kisses. He kept himself only to her and never told dirty jokes or had pornography in the house. He never cursed in front of her — or us. He treated her like a lady at all times.

My mother comported herself likewise. She dressed modestly and modeled the same kind of respect for my father as he had given her, during our formative years.

B) Teaching. My mother carefully taught me, "Jackie, no man who ever hits a woman is a man at all. A gentleman treats every woman like a lady. A gentleman relates to his wife with respect at all times. He never insults or yells at her. He never curses in the hearing of any woman. Intercourse outside of marriage is forbidden, not because there is anything wrong with sex. But, because sex is holy and clean and good, God has reserved it as a special gift between husband and wife only. Never sexually defile a woman, Jack. God holds men responsible to protect the virtue of all women." My father modeled what my mother taught, and that wrote it into my heart. Their teaching and modeling built boundaries in me I cannot pass to this day (see the first four chapters of Proverbs in this regard).

Bad modeling and teaching destroy all those positive attributes. Violence and disrespect between parents result in children's inability to respect the personhood of others. Immodest behavior (such as exposure of sexual organs to the opposite sex) makes it impossible to cherish the holiness of one's own body and others'. Illicit sex witnessed, or known about, implants varying degrees of incapacity to hold marriage vows sacred. Molestation destroys self-respect and the sanctity of one's own sexuality.

Nearly every case of sexual sins or dysfunction has at root bad modeling and/or teaching. Many cases also have roots of sexual abuse. Wise counselors will uncover and heal all bad roots in relation to how parents behaved towards each other and what they taught or failed to teach.

3) *Early sexual experiences badly handled by parents and/or family.*

A) "Playing doctor." If a parent catches children pulling down underwear and examining one another, he or she can make the experience either one of good learning or a root for trouble from then on! Good parenting at such times does not get emotional and above all does not become denigrating. Children are naturally curious and initially quite uninhibited. If a parent, on a first occasion, simply takes the child aside and teaches about the holiness and privateness of the body and warns not to do that again, a great deal more than words has been taught. Healthy attitudes are *caught*, not *taught*. If second and third instances happen, teaching can be repeated, followed by the loving and appropriate discipline we would administer for any other kind of disobedience.

Bad parenting occurs when parents are threatened about their own parenting or are governed by a religious rather than a Christian spirit. If they shout at the children, or hurl accusations, such as, "You're a naughty little boy/girl!" Or, "Bad! Bad! Bad! That's nasty," their children can't limit such accusations to the inappropriateness of their behavior. They apply "nasty" and "bad" to their own bodies and to sex itself. From then on, all natural wholesome sexual feelings will become tinged with nastiness and sinfulness. That later creates the dynamic of repression and expression which results in addictive and compulsive sexual behavior in born-anew adults.

B) Fondling of genital organs. All children need to explore their private parts and the concomitant sensations. It is normal for children to pass through phases or degrees of discovery. When teaching and modeling and discipline are bad (as outlined in A above), children become stuck in addictive, compulsive fondling of their own and others' genitals.

C) Accidental exposures. A child may happen into the bedroom while parents are exposed or sexually involved, or observe a parent of the opposite sex nude in the shower. Again, wise behavior and teaching will turn such experiences to blessing, but prudery based on negative attitudes about the body and bad teaching and modeling instill repressed desires for more illicit "sight-seeing."

D) Parental potty training and instruction about hygiene. My mother frankly and sensitively taught me about keeping my penis and testicles clean and dry, how to wipe myself, etc. And when my little sister was born and I saw that she urinated differently, Mom carefully taught me how and why little girls "go to the potty differently from little boys." No taboos or nastiness were attached to any bodily functions. But we in Elijah House have had to counsel many whose experiences in childhood set up both compulsive attractions and aversions.

Molestation, incest and rape.

Paula's book, *Healing Victims of Sexual Abuse* (especially the second chapter, "The Depths of Devastation"), fully documents the destruction of character and personality wrought by molestation, incest and rape. Nothing is more harmful to any person. Such woundings, however, result in promiscuity and marital sexual dysfunction more often than in voyeurism, pornography, fantasy and masturbation. Sexually abused people do not see sex as compellingly desirable nor as something which enlists rebellious desires to explore the forbidden. They may trash themselves due to ravaged self-esteem and unsatisfied hungers for loving touches. But they are usually not compelled by inordinate prurient (lewd, lascivious) desires.

5) *Sexual sins and dysfunctions in the ancestral heritage.*

Many who came to us caught in addictive and compulsive sexual behavior were found to have parents and grandparents who also suffered sexual dysfunctions, sinful behaviors, and detrimental attitudes and theologies. Sexual problems are inherited in the same three ways other problems are: 1) through the genes, physically, by inheritance of propensities to think and feel and act; 2) by modeling; and 3) by the law of sowing and reaping (Gal. 6:7; see Chapter 13, "Generational Sin," in *Healing the Wounded Spirit*). The three are usually aggravated by the presence of "familiars," demons appointed by Satan to watch over families to impel them into whatever weaknesses may present opportunities. Counselors should routinely check family histories when ministering to sexually entrapped people.

6) *Childhood influences and experiences among neighbors and family other than parents.*

I remember a time when I was about four years old. An older cousin came to visit and took me to an abandoned chicken coop. I couldn't understand why he kissed my penis. He thought it was something special to do. It repulsed me. I always remembered it. But Paula and I have ministered to hundreds whose relatives or friends involved them far more fully in illicit sexual activities, which created subliminal drives to repeat them as teens and adults. Cousins and friends in childhood frequently find forbidden games to play. For example, finding ways to watch older cousins undress, or mutual masturbation, entering into fellatio (oral sex performed upon a man), anal copulation ("sodomizing"), or bestiality, especially on farms. Children can invent hundreds of ways to experiment sexually. As we said in the beginning, most young people pass through such experiences as mere phases to look back on as adults and chuckle about. Such experiences become addictive and compulsive when parents wrongly handle discovery and discipline or so shame and wound their children that they cannot pass through to wholesome maturity. Counselors should examine their clients' childhood experiences, attempting to discern whether these were causal or only ancillary to the present problem, praying forgiveness and healing in any case.

7) *Influence of public school teachers, pastors and Sunday school teachers.*

Hundreds of times in our thirty years in counseling, Paula and I have found that childhood molestation or other sexually negative activities by teachers and pastors have caused sexual dysfunctions or sinfully compelling urges in born-anew Christians. These also need to be taken care of by counseling and prayer.

Voyeurism and Pornography

Voyeurism and pornography are latent in every human being. We are all tempted to want to see what is forbidden. The question we address now is, "How best can we heal it?"

Simple Steps for Healing

1) *Admit the problem.* Most addicts to voyeurism and pornography keep it hidden — even from themselves, like alcoholics, refusing to recognize that they are out of control, trapped by something greater than their power to resist. As alcoholics must take the first step of admitting what they are if they are to begin to get well, so addicts

to voyeurism and pornography must recognize their powerlessness in the flesh to stop. (See the appendix for lists of organizations which offer help to the sexually addicted.) Friends and counselors must encourage them to face facts squarely. The problem most often is that neither friends nor relatives know about it until discovery brings disgrace — or if they are somewhat aware, they remain ignorant of the gripping nature and extent of the addiction. Therefore, let any reader who has been involved in voyeurism or pornography hear this advice: Don't try to handle it by yourself! Humble yourself to talk to friends or a counselor. Perhaps you are not addicted — but don't make that determination by yourself. Be humble enough to let others discern and minister to you — before it does become compulsively addictive.

A word to friends and counselors: don't belittle or take lightly any discovery that someone you know occasionally succumbs to voyeurism or pornography! Voyeurism and pornography can become quickly addictive, especially in performance-oriented religious people. Confront, tactfully but insistently, until your loved one can ferret out the root causes and find full deliverance from both the cause and the habit.

2) *Search the childhood for roots.*

Wise people never try to uncover roots by themselves (Prov. 11:14, 15:22, etc.). Counselors and friends should look into whether performance orientation has made the person uptight and overly self-controlled, searching especially for fearful religious taboos in the childhood. (Religion can be defined as men and women searching for God, trying to please God. Faith is God finding mankind, God saving and comforting men and women. Religiosity is filled with striving and fear. Faith is filled with rest and joy. A religious spirit is deadly to our emotional health.)

Enable forgiveness. Most importantly, enable the person to forgive himself. Counselors must teach sexually addicted people how to look upon themselves with compassion and understanding, which will help to restore self-esteem.

The counselee must come to see that he/she actually seeks something other than looking on others' nakedness, that he has merely identified the satisfaction of his hungers in that unfulfilling habit. The person may actually be impelled by a childish need to rebel, to individuate from domineering parents, or to defile the opposite sex because of repressed hatreds, and so on. (Inherited factors may be part of the problem.) Once the counselee sees the actual reasons for his behavior, the habit loses its compelling force. All such structures within the old self need to find fulness of death on the cross. New habits of thinking and feeling in Christ should be built by worship and prayer, by Bible reading and by service to others.

3) *Sometimes deliverance from demons is involved.*

Don't jump to conclusions or administer deliverance too soon even if demonization is surely indicated or confirmed. Hatred of the habit, repentance, and the destruction of root causes must accompany deliverance, or the last state of the person will become seven times worse (Luke 11:24-26). Unclean spirits can use hidden factors in the heart and mind to drive tendencies into compulsions. A counselor may have to bind demonic forces (silently or aloud) even to begin to counsel with effect. Wise counselors learn how to throttle the effectiveness of demons without casting them completely away until the person has been made strong enough and becomes sufficiently informed to withstand demons' attempts to reenter. Then deliverance can be complete and joyful — without relapse.

4) *Learn to sublimate and make restitution.*

After healing and deliverance, temptations will recur. Old habits, even when stripped of their power, can continue to act up. When a man quits pulling a belfry rope, the bell may continue to ring for a while, but if he leaves it alone, it will slow down and stop on its own. Just so, when roots have been dealt with but urges still rise simply from habit, counselees should be taught to check impulses, pray to release burdens to Jesus, and then concentrate on something useful and helpful for someone else. If an old practice can convince us that it has renewed life, it will throw us back into the dynamic of suppression and expression which revives and increases its power. We need to reckon it as dead and redirect our energies toward something rewarding and wholesome. That old "bell" will soon cease its clanging.

Counselors can assign tasks which involve the person in helping others. Doing things for others restores self-esteem and helps make restitution for whatever damages the habit has done. No one can earn his own redemption, but the Lord knows that requiring us to serve others restores and heals us even more than it does those we help. Perhaps the best restitution is to help heal those who have been overcome by similar sinful habits and, where practical, those we may have injured.

Fantasy and Masturbation

Masturbation is common to all. I remember hearing a well-known family counselor say that 97% admit they have masturbated — and the other 3% are liars! Pre-teens experiment with their bodily sensations and soon learn the excitement of stimulation and the sense of release which climax provides. Teenagers need physical release, but Christian conscience and teaching prohibit intercourse. That puts a strain on the body — designed to express sexually but unable to, sometimes for years after the body is ready.

Masturbation is not specifically forbidden in the Scriptures. I have not been able to find references to it in the Law, yea or nay. Nor has anyone else, to my knowledge, without twisting or stretching words. Many, having read our references to masturbation in the section on sexual sins in *The Transformation of the Inner Man,* have written to us, angry that we did not castigate it as sin. But a true servant of the Lord can be adamant and certain only where Scripture is unequivocal, and must remain silent wherever the Bible is moot, no matter what his personal preferences may be.

Masturbation becomes sinful when other factors combine with it, such as fantasy. Fantasy is not in itself evil. To be able to visualize and daydream is one of God's greatest gifts to mankind. Fantasy is one of God's best gifts for enabling creativity. From this gift many wondrous inventions and scientific marvels have come. But any gift of God can be perverted to wrongful uses. When the power of fantasizing is coupled with masturbation, the sin of fornication or adultery is involved. "You have heard that it was said, 'YOU SHALL NOT COMMIT ADULTERY'; but I say to you, that everyone who *looks* on a woman to lust for her has committed adultery with her already in his heart" (Matt. 5: 27-28).

Whenever it is discovered that a client has been active in masturbation, the counselor should check to see whether fantasy has also been involved. If so, repentance, forgiveness, admonition and teaching must follow. The habit of fantasizing must be broken. Frequently, the client will have to be made aware that fantasizing is different from mere daydreaming, which can be solitary and innocuous. But because we are corporate, fantasizing always defiles the other person and is thus sinful.

Masturbation also becomes sin through idolatry. Married couples know that the aftermath of sexual climax is peace and restfulness flowing throughout the nervous system. When tension is a constant in the life-style of young people, it does not take them long to identify masturbation and orgasm as a way to find release and relaxation. They learn that every time they achieve climax, their bodies and emotions settle into euphoric rest. The longing for release and rest, and the identification of masturbation as the way to find it, can then create addiction.

I have ministered to a number of successful pastors and leaders who could not understand why they continued to be bedeviled by the compulsion to masturbate. Most said their spouses were fully adequate as lovers. That made the compulsion even more confusing to them. They hated themselves for it but could not stop. Again, the power of the dynamic of suppression and expression increased the force of the habit the more they struggled against it. The actual sin was idolatry. They had learned to find by masturbating what they should have obtained through prayer and worship. Most of these leaders, as adults, had developed fully satisfying abilities to pray and to enter into worship, but the addiction continued because the earlier built-in "track" of equating masturbation with release and rest was an unconscious mechanism which had never been brought to death on the cross.

Normally, people build the habit of masturbating long before receiving Jesus as their Lord and Savior. Usually, following conversion, the presence of the Lord so fills the heart with peace that for a while there is no need for any other kind of relief. But after those first few euphoric months, most Christians begin to go through desert times in their devotional life, usually at the same time pressures and tensions increase. That may cause the Christian to regress emotionally. Since he can't find release through prayer, and tensions threaten to undo his equilibrium, it is a simple step to return to finding release through masturbation. Disgust, fear and guilt may then lock him into the dynamic of suppression and expression, which turns the revivified habit more and more into a compulsion — which further mystifies and confuses him.

Counselors must avoid heaping condemnation on the person. Excessive guilt in this case will not find its way to the cross and so effect freedom. Rather, feelings of guilt will most likely become sidetracked into striving, thus adding more fuel to the fire. Teaching and explanation can help the person to understand how idolatry is the real sin, and how suppression and fleshly striving combine to increase the addiction. Forgiveness for idolatry should be expressed. But then the counselee should be taught to relax about the habit. *The need for physical release is not the same as the need for emotional release and rest.* Counselees must come to see that those two needs have become wrongfully joined together and that emotional release can be found in other and better ways.

The compulsion to masturbate is thus a bomb which must be defused first by understanding. I tell unmarried people, if once in a while they masturbate, not to put themselves under guilt and bondage about it. Their bodies need that physical release. I teach them to forgive themselves if they feel it is necessary (especially if fantasizing has also been involved), but then to forget about it and go on living. Many have returned to testify to me that it worked; they no longer struggle with it as a compulsion. They are free of it as a habit. They may still do it occasionally just because the body needs that intermittent physical release, but they no longer have to use it to find emotional relaxation from problems.

Married people who still masturbate need help to identify the childhood patterns of emotional release through masturbation, and bring them to death on the cross, and then to learn to talk out their problems, pray with their spouses, and enjoy more fully the glory of marital sex. But an additional factor needs to be addressed here: some may have established habits of failing to be corporate. The habit of masturbating may have established a secondary habit of seeking self-gratification in sex. That can cause them not to truly meet and interact with their mate in the act of intercourse. They have so long practiced self-gratification that they may in effect be masturbating during intercourse — merely using the spouse to find release for themselves. They may never have learned how to meet and refresh the other in love-play. Wise counselors will investigate to find whether and to what extent that may be the case. Forgiveness and reconciliation between the couple will be needed, along with careful teaching about how to become truly corporate in their marriage, and thus to refresh and fulfil one another.

Fantasy simply must be stopped. Seldom is fantasy so addictive that will power coupled with prayer cannot quickly end the habit. Fantasy is supplemental to the physical compulsion of masturbation. It is not causal, and usually is not hooked into the dynamic of suppression and expression. However, if the Christian does not come to realize the seriousness of it as a sin (as a defilement of others) and so decide to detest and quit it, he will not find it easy to turn about in his tracks. One or two sessions of counseling and prayer are usually enough to end the fantasy part of the addiction to masturbation.

Sometimes, masturbation has also become subconsciously connected to other factors, such as teenage rebellion, the need to punish parents by acting badly, or addiction to pornography and voyeurism. In such cases, the counselor needs to identify and separate the various components, and to help the counselee see how each got started and comprehend how they interact. Thus the counselee gradually recovers control of himself, and learns to fight his own battles where they really are, instead of being caught up in futile self-recriminations.

Finally, the client needs to be taught how to find true emotional release through prayer and the sharing of his heart with others. If skills of communication and prayer are not established, the client will regress into inappropriate ways of finding emotional release, most likely through whatever habit gripped him before.

Section 2:
Historical, Theological
and Cultural Causes

Preface to Section Two

Some historical, cultural and theological causes for sexual sins have already been touched upon in previous chapters. I repeat them for two reasons: first, to teach in fuller and clearer detail; second, to enable teachers (and possibly editors of magazines) to lift out chapters as complete units. For that purpose, each chapter in the book has been designed to stand on its own.

It is difficult to separate historical from cultural and theological causes. They intertwine. Historical developments greatly affect culture and theology; cultural and theological changes alter the course of history. For the purpose of these chapters, I list under historical causes those events which I believe have most affected our Western culture and theology, and thus Christian behavior. In like manner, I attempt to describe the cultural and theological trends which I believe have most affected historical events and our ability to think and act in Christ-like ways.

No such discussion can be exhaustive in only three chapters. Therefore, I have tried to condense my remarks to revelations we can do something about. My aim is not merely scholastic, but it involves pragmatic transformation and redemption. What I sketch here will, I hope, spark Christian researchers and scholars to develop more fully the knowledge our colleges and seminaries desperately need in order to discipline future leaders' minds and hearts, so that the next generation will not have to struggle through the flood of rampant sexual sin we have seen.

6

Historical Causes for Sexual Sins

The greatest historical cause for sexual sins among Christians and non-Christians alike is the destruction of family roles and relationships which began with the advent of the Industrial Revolution. Before then, all mankind lived in an agrarian and merchant society. Sons and daughters worked alongside their fathers and mothers on the farm or in the shop. Craftsmen such as carpenters, clockmakers, potters, smiths and wheelwrights built their homes behind or above their workshops. It was the same for merchants.

Wives and daughters were not far from husbands' and fathers' elbows. They knew what their menfolk were doing and often worked alongside them.

A man's work and destiny were interwoven with his home and family. Ingrained in every father's mentality was that he should deposit his skills and principles in his children by word and example. His philosophy of life was important; his faith was corporate and transmittable, not merely a matter of his own personal redemption but that of his family also.

Father was the general upon the field; his presence and oversight left scant room for immoral escapades — and the lack of today's labor-saving devices left little energy or time for them. His comradeship strengthened his children's spirits with the capacity to stand morally. (We are speaking of Christian families; closeness meant also that immoral and pagan fathers had that same opportunity to contaminate their children's lives.)

Wives knew their husbands' hearts and shared their burdens fully. They labored as a team, both at work and in the raising of their children. A wife's heart refined her husband's philosophy and faith, gentled it and represented it to their children. She knew her place (in the best sense of that word), both in his heart as his wife and in her role as a mother.

Honoring and obeying one's parents (Deut. 5:16) was the very structure of the way life was lived. Without obedience, most families would have failed to survive. And since the children worked alongside their parents, they knew their parents' hearts, and the parents knew them. *There was no generation gap.* Generation gaps are the result of the Industrial Revolution. Parents and children before that time lived in harness together, both at work and in their thinking.

Though what has been described so far may seem a bit idealistic (mankind's sinful nature being what it is), the point is that family structures existed which made parents' influence sharp and clear. Faith was not something merely individual. Family closeness meant that whatever possessed the parents' hearts gripped the children's as well. Minds might disagree and choose their own opinions, but there was no escaping the impact of one another's hearts and life-styles. Parents stamped their natures upon their children's lives by the necessities of daily survival together.

Today all that has changed. With the advent of the Industrial Revolution, fathers have increasingly worked away from the home. Wives and children rarely labor alongside the men. Few fathers today feel it incumbent upon them to pass along their skills of craftsmanship. Children may know almost nothing about what their father does, and they are not part of that doing. Fathers are gone long hours from the home. Children no longer know their father's heart. The father's philosophy and faith have taken second place to the mother's, which may or may not be the same. Public and Sunday school teachers now fill the place fathers once held, both in the minds and hearts of children. Fathers tend to yield their responsibilities of nurture and admonition to mothers and preachers.

Husbands and fathers now inhabit two worlds. The world of ambition and craftsmanship is no longer tied into the home, requiring the children's assistance. Now, men usually feel they need to succeed in the marketplace rather than at home. Family most often takes second place to the career. A man may feel confident at work, proud of his abilities. He knows what buttons to push. He knows how to make things happen. But when he comes home, he often has insufficient first-hand data to make whatever decisions are thrust upon him.

Relating to his wife and children requires an entirely different set of sensitivities and skills than he has found successful at work. He sometimes feels like a foreigner at the helm of a strange ship with a crew that speaks an alien language. His work-world therefore looms as a great temptation, something to flee to where he can feel competent and successful, where he can congratulate himself that he is in control. Life in the family-world often seems grossly out of control, and that feeling threatens any man's sense of who he is. Consequently his work-world, rather than his wife and family, comes to be thought of as the place of restoration. That fact alone sets him up for affairs with whomever shares his time and emotions at work.

His wife too often becomes the sole expert in the home. She knows the details he has had no time for. She knows the children's hearts; he doesn't. She lives in a feminine world of sensitivities and emotions which have no place in a workaday world. (At work, he must not say the obvious, or he will be looked upon as stupid or boring. One must not say what everyone knows and what has been said before.) At home, life operates on a totally opposite basis! His wife knows she has prepared a nice meal, but she needs him to compliment her anyway. He has said hundreds of times that he loves her and that she looks nice. To say it again is repetitive and seemingly unnecessary. But she couldn't care less about repetition and the obvious. She needs to hear those words.

She talks on and on about "trivia" which to her are not at all meaningless, and, if he only knew, are not meaningless to him either. But he has his mind on multi-million dollar decisions, operations, technicalities, etc. The little emotional concerns of daily living hardly seem as gripping or exciting, or vital to financial survival, as the "important" matters he may be carrying home in his heart and mind.

Thus he abdicates his role as priest, head and father and no longer really knows his wife and family, nor she and they him. He is continually seduced to the familiar arena of his ambitions, abandoning the raising of the children to his wife's seemingly greater competence and interest. Eventually he comes to a position of wanting to have a wife and children, but not in actual fact wanting to be intimately married and corporately invested in fathering his children.

Recently, more and more women have wanted to escape the home to have careers. Or to try to have careers and children. Children in such homes are often relegated to day care and/or boarding schools, bereft of both parents for long periods of time — with consequent destructions to their character and moral fortitude.

The advent of the industrial age has thus resulted in at least two major sources of immorality in our society, affecting Christians as well, unfortunately. First, the withdrawal of fathers from their God-ordained parental role has horribly damaged the ability of their children to stand morally:

> Behold, I am going to send you Elijah the prophet before the coming of the great and terrible day of the Lord. And he will restore the hearts of the fathers to their children, and the hearts of the children to their fathers, lest I come and smite the land with a curse. (Mal. 4:5-6)

The curse is already here, through rising crime rates, drugs, separations and divorces, fornications and adulteries, etc. ad nauseam. (See *Healing the Wounded Spirit*, Chapter 5, "The Slumbering Spirit.") The curse comes from two great voids in children's lives: A) The lack of appropriate paternal discipline. Mothers' discipline helps, but it is paternal discipline which structures morality into children's hearts, teaches limits and builds in the ability to deny selfish desires. Generations upon generations now suffer deficient moral self-control due to insufficient parental discipline, especially that of the father.

B) The lack of paternal teaching and modeling of moral principles has almost totally destroyed comprehension of the altruistic reasons for moral laws. The laws of God are actually guidelines to show how love acts (and doesn't act) in relationships. But to countless multitudes who have never learned to sacrifice in love for others, laws only thwart their desires and egocentric self-expressions. Children who have never been patiently taught, hour by hour, working beside their fathers and mothers for the good of others, have almost no grasp of the purpose and intent of civil or biblical laws! They have never learned to love law for righteousness' sake. They have little respect for law and order for others' sake. To whatever degree they do obey moral laws, it is because they fear being caught. (When they are sure they can get away undetected, they do whatever they want.) Thus, even among many born-anew Christians, the structures of character which enable the Holy Spirit to hold us to the track of righteousness are simply not there. When pressures mount, whatever has been built by parents in the moral character takes over and tells in the end whether Christians stand or fall.

Lack of parental nurture, especially from fathers, has caused many, Christians and non-Christians, to have a slumbering spirit. Affection awakens and directs the personal spirits of children in the art of relationship (see the aforementioned chapter on "Slumbering Spirits"). Adults who lacked affection in childhood cannot sustain intimacy in primary relationships. Without affection in childhood, adults lack a true working conscience. Thus immorality beckons without effective checks. Children who are not touched often enough wither in their personal spirits (like plants left unwatered in a hot sun) and grow to be adults who cannot function properly in any kind of relationship. That leaves great unsatisfied hungers and lonelinesses. Unmet needs coupled with a lack of conscience add up to affairs and adulteries, especially since affairs seem to offer intimacy without the cost of commitment.

Lack of paternal priesthood in the family has meant that children in such families grow to become adults who have trouble relating to God in real life. When they are born anew, they learn to worship corporately — but only by copying what others do. They have no built-in ways for carrying on a private devotional life with the Lord. And they possess no practical spiritual skills for handling by prayer life's daily little problems, to say nothing of the major crises. They may remember to say table graces, but they have acquired no abilities for mediating forgiveness among family members through counseling and prayer, no knowledge of how to lay hands on their children for healing, no awareness of their duty to pray a blessing daily for family members or how to do it should they become aware. They fail to protect their children through daily prayers of intercession.

Consequently, their children grow to adulthood with no awareness of their own priestly callings and functions as parents, or the capacities to perform them. The result is twofold: first, adult children of such families have virtually no skills for personal redemption of family problems or for finding refreshment from the tensions of daily living. That leaves them vulnerable to those who seem to understand them and to offer the comfort they lack at home, thus leading to affairs and adulteries.

Second, their faith becomes divorced from reality in their's and their children's lives. No one in the family knows in real terms how to apply the blood and cross and the resurrection life of Jesus to the hearts of family members. The result is that the righteousness of God finds few channels for expression in daily family living — or anywhere else. The final result is that immorality runs increasingly rampant from generation to generation — until someone relearns how to live the faith in the family where it counts, pays the price of self-discipline to stop the cycle of degeneration, and rebuilds Christian practices into his family.

The Antidote

There is no other antidote than becoming determined to establish unbending priorities. As we said earlier, the Lord spoke unequivocally to Paula and me. He had called us to be among those who help restore the office of the prophet, among those who help to restore the family, and among those who pioneer the healing of the inner man and who try to raise up body ministry in the Church. But He told us that more important than any or all of those tasks was the raising of our six children! He showed us that a man could write great books, become an industrial magnate, discover scientific breakthroughs or create inventions that would help all of mankind. But none of those things would be as important as whatever children God sends his way. Discoveries, inventions, books, careers — all will eventually pass away and be forgotten. But a man's children will live forever!

Folk wisdom tells us, "You can't take it with you" (when you die). That's only partly true. Every possession will have to be left behind. But every bit of character you have acquired and every scrap of knowledge which has entered your mind will go with you to heaven! Likewise, everything built by parents into their children's character and personality will be tested by the fires of the Lord and of life, and whatever has been built upon the rock of Jesus' nature will survive throughout eternity!

> For no man can lay a foundation other than
> the one which is laid, which is Jesus Christ. Now
> if any man builds upon the foundation with

gold, silver, precious stones, wood, hay, straw, each man's work will become evident; for the day will show it, because it is to be revealed with fire; and the fire itself will test the quality of each man's work. If any man's work which he has built upon it remains, he shall receive a reward. If any man's work is burned up, he shall suffer loss; but he himself shall be saved, yet so as through fire. (1 Cor. 3:11-15)

Do not our divorce statistics manifest the fires of life, burning up by painful loss the false lessons some parents have written into their children? If fathers really understood this, what man would allow his eternal work to be burned up? (The grace of Christ would take him to heaven, but he would receive no reward.) And what man could stand to see the destruction of his children's welfare before he goes there? The same applies to mothers. (Not every loss is due to poor parenting; sometimes a well-taught child marries a "mess" and suffers the fires the in-laws are reaping.) If only more parents understood the importance of who they are to their children, and of their calling to build into their children with gold (the nature of God and wisdom), silver (biblical, heavenly knowledge) and precious stones (gems of Christ-like character), what a difference that would make in the Church and in the world!

God has commissioned us parents to put that eternal deposit into our children's characters. Nothing else we do is such an eternal work. There will never be another person exactly like the child God gives to a man and woman. There will not be another voice track, fingerprint, personality or character like that little one in all the universe, in all of eternity! Birthing and raising our children is perhaps the only eternal work we will ever do! We may have an impact on others and may deposit some beautiful and lasting things in them. But with no others will we ever be in that distinct and peculiar position of being the primary agents to shape a soul for eternity! Is it not worth sacrificing every other hope and ambition to accomplish?

By the grace of God, and perhaps largely due to that early teaching from the Lord, all six of our children are born-anew Christians, along with their spouses. Our eldest son, Loren, and his wife, Beth, minister to all the rest of the family as pastor and wife, and they teach alongside us in Elijah House. Ami and her husband, Tony, teach Sunday school in Loren's church. Tony is editing this book for me. Mark and Maureen have recently moved here from Florida where he ministered for several years as a Christian counselor. Maureen contributed significantly in that ministry. Mark is now one of our Elijah House counselors and will be ordained in his brother's church. John and Marty belong to the same church and make a strong Christian witness as they have opportunity. Tim is a high school music teacher who, assisted by his wife, Victoria, leads worship in a church in Montana. They provide leadership for youth in Christian camps and retreats. They will shortly return to graduate school to increase their effectiveness. Andrea has married Randy, the leader of a university Baptist student ministries group, and she sings as part of its traveling ministry team. All of our children and their spouses stand on their own feet before the Lord, skilled in the priestly functions which heal and sustain family relationships.

We owe all that to the Lord's insistence that those children are our first priority in life! They are what they are by grace of God, but grace must find vessels to act in. We plead with the Body of Christ: pour your time and energies where it counts, where you and you only have been called — into your children's lives. Spend whatever time and energy it costs to learn the skills no school can teach — how to minister the grace of our Lord Jesus Christ in daily family living. *Nothing else is as important as that work God appointed you to when He gave you those children!*

The Second Historical Cause

The second greatest historical cause of sexual sins among

Christians today is the advent of technology, which first began to impact our culture drastically in the nineteenth century. Scientific advances have set us free from drudgery and have afforded us comforts and conveniences unheard of in previous centuries. Medical discoveries have delivered us from diseases which heretofore routinely killed or disfigured millions. But the fruits of science have been a mixed blessing. Technology has also caused two generations to live under the threat of instant annihilation.

Beginning in the nineteenth century, Satan tried to use the onslaught of scientific discoveries and successes to make Christians ashamed to stand upon the Word of God. Scholars began to look for empirical, scientific bases for knowledge rather than the simple belief that God has spoken once for all. Scientific scholarship into archaeology and the languages of the Bible was and is extremely valuable. But historically the rise of modernistic scholarship coincided with the birth of theological liberalism. Some began to use science to undermine the Bible rather than to encourage belief in its verities. Consequently, thousands of preachers and teachers have graduated from certain seminaries trained to confuse and undo the faith of their congregations. Many Christians now no longer believe that God's Word and His Laws are absolute or relevant for today's living.

But the damage has been deeper and much more perilous than that. When men began to question the veracity of the Bible and, therefore, the wisdom of Almighty God and His eternal Laws, there remained no bounds for the questionings of carnal mentality, no humility of mind among men. "If God has not spoken, then I become my own god; I make up my own rules." "I don't see that every law of God is eternal and unchangeable, nor do I recognize that every one of His laws is His loving gift for our guidance." "If I don't understand why God has given a commandment, I don't need to because I know better than God what is best for me — and for everyone else!"

A friend of ours to whom we had sent many for

counseling decided she needed more formal training and so went back to school for secular education in counseling. (There is nothing wrong with sharpening our skills through formal training so long as we hold firmly to our faith.) But along the way, she lost her underpinnings in the Word of God and found in humanistic philosophy what seemed to be kinder wisdom.

Not realizing what had become of her faith, we sent a confessed homosexual to her for healing. He wrote to us with great grief that she had told him homosexuality is a fully acceptable life-style and had referred him to a "gay" group where he might find fellowship! It devastated him to be told that he didn't need healing and he should expect to continue to live that way! She thought she was being kind! "All those scriptures prohibiting homosexuality are just Old Testament thoughts of mortal men, and of course, in this enlightened age, we have become wiser and kinder than that!"

Such is the seductive arrogance of Satan; such is his perverted "wisdom."

We also see that arrogance and "wisdom" in more than sixteen million murders by abortion (in America alone). God had clearly said, "You shall not murder (Deut. 5:17)." But it is obviously "kinder and wiser" to allow women to choose what is right for their bodies (though none of us possesses the wisdom to make that kind of decision). And if that means flushing a mere "piece of extraneous material" from the womb, who cares?! Satan has found new ways to cloud the minds of many while asking the same age-old question, "Did God really say not to. . .?"

The denomination in which I grew up established a committee (as did many other liberal, mainline denominations) to examine what church members should think about the sexual revolution and what ought to be the sexual standards for modern Christians. Thinking the question was at all open to debate reveals the sickness among them!! There is nothing to discuss; one has only to read His Word. His commandments are absolute for every age. They allow no adaptation. They are eternally relevant. They will continue beyond the destruction of this earth into eternity:

> Do not think that I came to abolish the Law or the Prophets; I did not come to abolish, but to fulfill. For truly I say to you, until heaven and earth pass away, not the smallest letter or stroke shall pass away from the Law, until all is accomplished. Whoever then annuls one of the least of these commandments, and so teaches others, shall be called least in the kingdom of heaven; but whoever keeps and teaches them, he shall be called great in the kingdom of heaven. (Matt. 5:17-19)

Tragically, many born-anew Christians who agree fully with what we've said are ignorant of how modernism and liberalism and new age thinking may have defiled their minds and hearts: their *minds* may believe in the truth of God's commands, but their *hearts* may not be able to keep their way any purer any more than unbelievers. I have seen this again and again as I've counseled Christians who are involved in sexual sins. They give constant lip-service to the truth of the Bible, but when it came right down to where decisions were made for honesty in business and morality in sex, the Word had not gripped their hearts at all!

The absoluteness of Law, the fear of God, the restraints of a mind gladly subject to God's statutes were not there in real terms!! We have not yet begun to realize the depths of the defilement in our thinking through modernism, liberalism and new-age mentality.

The Third Historical Cause

This leads us to the third great historical cause for sexual — and other — sins among born-anew Christians today: *Modernism, liberalism and new-age mentality have nearly destroyed our American jurisprudence system.* When men did away with the sure guidelines of God's eternal laws and thought they could be kinder and wiser than God, our justice system was left with nothing but the foolishness of men as its basis.

Recently, a friend informed me of the following case: a man phoned a police station to admit he was the serial rapist for whom they had been searching. The police brought him to the station where he wrote out a full confession for all his crimes. There was no question of his guilt. The judge set him free because when the police picked him up in their patrol car he had somehow been deprived of his rights!

Another instance: a motorcyclist on drugs crossed the median and ran head-on into a van driven by a woman. The crash broke his leg. The investigating officer gave him several citations and completely exonerated her. There was nothing she could have done to avoid being hit by him. There was no question of his guilt. Now he is suing the woman because her van deprived him of his ability to work for a period of time! The lawyer defending the woman expects that the cyclist will win a judgment against her! The real reason for the suit is that without it the cyclist would lose his insurance or have to pay exorbitant rates. Legal fees are driving her into bankruptcy.

Who has not heard of instances of citizens who defended their property from theft being successfully sued by the robber? Or of policemen being suspended because they used their weapons to defend citizens' rights?

These are but a few of the countless miscarriages of justice any of us could cite. Certainly there have been some instances where the forces of law and order have been overzealous, but many law officers are disillusioned and disgusted because "the system" sets criminals free on the merest of technicalities which somehow "deprived them of their rights." Parole boards frequently release unrepentant criminals who go right back to a life of crime. The rights of honest citizens are trampled underfoot in a society ruled by human mentality bereft of the pillars of justice provided by the eternal laws of God.

Paula and I recently spoke in Singapore. Residents there said there is almost no crime in Singapore! When we asked why, we were told that there are no plea bargainings, no long court delays, no getting off scot-free on technicalities. For instance, they reported that a woman can walk safely anywhere in the country day or night without fear of rape. The penalty for one count of rape is thirty-two years in prison, with twenty-four strokes of the *raton*. The *raton* is a wand soaked in ammonia. Each stroke pierces into the flesh and the ammonia causes such pain that the recipient passes out! Rapists receive one stroke per year for twenty-four years, and then serve eight more years before being released.

Some thought the use of the *raton* was too brutal. They discontinued its use for a time, only to see a dramatic increase in rape! The perpetrators were more afraid of the raton than of thirty-two years in prison!

Doubtless I will receive letters of rebuke for reporting that practice, because despite the disclaimer I add here, some will think I advocate using that kind of thing in America. (I don't.) The point is that before we became more concerned about protecting criminals than the innocent, our laws carried some toughness, and the crime rate was nowhere near where it is today. We have reaped and will reap even more because we have substituted man's ideas of kindness for God's laws.

Tough laws *are* kindness, even to protect the criminally minded from themselves. I challenge readers to study what the Word of God says concerning penalties for sin, both in the Old Testament and in the New. When Satan successfully dislodged the Word of God from its hold on men's minds, he could make God's laws seem irrelevant and unkind to an age made proud of its own foolish thoughts and thus cause us to reap destruction in our society.

> For even though they knew God, they did
> not honor Him as God, or give thanks; but they
> became futile in their speculations, and their

foolish heart was darkened. Professing to be wise, they became fools. (Rom. 1:21 & 22)

I suggest reading the remainder of Romans 1 for an eye-popping understanding of why our society has fallen to such abominable crimes as those that beset us today!

When people see crimes going unpunished and the wicked flourishing, belief in the moral laws of God is undermined. The message to sinners is that there will be little or no punishment for any crime they do. For example, on a trip to a convention a man may slip into an unpremeditated adultery. He feels bad and is terrified that his wife might find out. But she believes his cover story. And the sky didn't fall on him. In fact, life seemed to go on much as usual. It is then easier to give in to temptation the next time, which he also seems to get away with.

The seeming lack of retribution for sin makes him wonder whether there are any "eternal, irrevocable laws" governing human behavior. But God's laws, specifically in this case the law of sowing and reaping (Gal. 6:7), are inexorable. When the inevitable destruction falls upon him for his sins (reaping often happens many years after the event), he may not connect the trouble with the real reason at all, wondering why such things should happen to him and his family. A holy fear of God and His Laws no longer acts with sufficient power to deter even Christians from sinning.

Our civil laws used to reflect their Judeo-Christian heritage. Homosexuality, fornication and adultery were all forbidden by civil law. And bans against pornography had not yet succumbed to foolish applications of the right of free speech. Now, though in most places God's laws can still be found in the civil law books, no one would even attempt an indictment for moral sins, much less expect to obtain a conviction. Why? Because the absoluteness and the wisdom of God's holy laws governing human behavior have been replaced in the minds of people by their own foolish thoughts. Therefore sexual sin runs rampant in the world. Born-anew

Christians find it hard to fight off because the bombardment of unrighteousness in our society continually erodes the heart's ability to hold to that which the renewed mind in Christ knows is true and right.

Though we say that the corruption of our legal system is a modern phenomenon through the advent of modernism and liberalism, for other reasons corruption through unbelief also destroyed justice in Israel in biblical times. Listen to the thunderings of Isaiah:

> For your hands are defiled with blood,
> And your fingers with iniquity;
> Your lips have spoken falsehood,
> Your tongue mutters wickedness.
> No one sues righteously and no one pleads honestly.
> They trust in confusion, and speak lies;
> They conceive mischief, and bring forth iniquity.
> They hatch adders' eggs and weave the spider's web;
> He who eats of their eggs dies,
> And from that which is crushed a snake breaks forth.
> Their webs will not become clothing,
> Nor will they cover themselves with their works;
> Their works are works of iniquity, And an act of violence is in their hands.
> Their feet run to evil,
> And they hasten to shed innocent blood;
> Their thoughts are thoughts of iniquity;
> Devastation and destruction are in their highways.
> They do not know the way of peace,
> And there is no justice in their tracks; They have made their paths crooked;
> Whoever treads on them does not know peace.

Therefore, justice is far from us,
And righteousness does not overtake us;
We hope for light, but behold, darkness;
For brightness, but we walk in gloom.
We grope along the wall like blind men,
We grope like those who have no eyes;
We stumble at midday as in the twilight,
Among those who are vigorous we are like
dead men.
All of us growl like bears,
And moan sadly like doves;
We hope for justice, but there is none,
For salvation, but it is far from us.
For our transgressions are multiplied before
Thee,
And our sins testify against us;
For our transgressions are with us,
And we know our iniquities;
Transgressing and denying the Lord,
And turning away from our God,
Speaking oppression and revolt,
Conceiving in and uttering from the heart
lying words.
And justice is turned back,
And righteousness stands far away;
For truth has stumbled in the street,
And uprightness cannot enter.
Yes, truth is lacking;
And he who turns aside from evil makes
himself a prey. (Isa. 59:3-15a)

The Fourth Historical Cause

The fourth great historical cause for sexual and other sins in our time is the birth of modern mass media. Instant news from radio and TV, and overnight information from newspapers, have made us instantly aware of the sins of leaders and laypeople. Movies, TV, VCR's, novels, short stories and magazines have displayed sinful ways like the flood poured out of Satan's mouth to overcome the woman who is the Church (Rev. 12:15). I mentioned this earlier, so let me just add that when one sees the impact of mass media, combined with liberal new-age thinking, the erosion of our justice system, and the consequent sapping of belief in the laws of God, it is no wonder that so many Christians succumb to sins! It takes a strong, secure Christian to stand for righteousness in an increasingly corrupted age.

Other Historical Causes

There are other historical causes: the effects of two world wars. The easing of divorce laws. The abolition of effective censorship. Greed in the marketplace. The rise in occult practices and satanic worship and the blindness and unbelief, especially among nominal Christians, concerning Satan and the demonic powers.

The onslaught of "gay" rights movements and their warped thinking. Out-of-balance feminist activities. Disillusionment with politicians, and the widespread acceptance throughout society of the philosophy that the end justifies the means. The erosion of the code of honor that a man should live by his word and would rather die than let it fall to the ground. (My Grandfather Potter was an Oklahoma rancher who concluded multi-thousand dollar deals with only a handshake, saying, "If that man's word isn't good, no amount of paper is going to hold him to it.")

The denigrating effect of pornography on what men think of women, to the point that men no longer feel that they are commissioned by God to protect every woman's honor. The removal of prayer from our schools. The public schools' substitution of the the bland emptinesses of "Dick, Jane and Spot" for the McGuffey Readers (which taught solid moral lessons). The effect the availability of abortions has had on sexual intercourse outside marriage.

But all of these and more can be traced to the destruction of belief in the Word of God, the loss of holy awe and respect for God's righteousness, and the defilements modernism and liberalism have wrought upon the thinking and consciences of men and women in this age.

Antidotes

I have listed many antidotes in previous chapters. I would sum them all up in one urgent plea: *if we do not have a prolonged, old-fashioned revival, I believe this nation and the world are doomed!* I say "old-fashioned" because the revivals of previous centuries carried with them fulsome repentance. They effected a return to moral and holy lifestyles sadly missing in what passes for revival today. Somehow our conversion experiences seem to lack the shuddering depth of revulsion against sin which stirred those who earlier fled to the altar of God.

The 1910 revival in Wales so changed the miners that the beasts hauling the ore cars wouldn't budge — they no longer heard the cursing they had come to associate with orders. At the same time, police in many American cities suddenly had so little to do, they formed barbershop quartets to pass the time. Those revivals changed the moral character of entire regions. Unfortunately, that is not so today.

Several years ago, Elijah House conducted a seminar on sexual problems. Every participant was born-anew. To open the proceedings, we handed out a survey list of forty-three questions. The participants were assured that total anonymity would protect the honesty of their answers. Among other questions, we asked whether they had committed fornication before marriage, and/or adultery afterwards. Over 50 percent admitted to fornication, the same for adultery; and most confessed to having committed both. Then we asked how many had committed the same sins *after* being born anew. Over 40 percent! *That meant that belief in Christ had effected only a ten per cent improvement in moral behavior!* In similar surveys since then the results have been the same. Somehow the holiness of our Lord Jesus Christ has not yet come to abide in the hearts of many of today's born-anew Christians!

There must come a weeping before God and a crying

out for true revival which can *truly* change the hearts of those who respond. As a counselor I know and teach that there must, after conversion, be a time of sanctification by daily death on the cross, but I also know unless their hearts are truly repentant and seeking to be made like Christ, men and women will not undergo the cost in pain to ferret out sin and die to it.

There must come a breaking. There must come a fire of love so deep that men can no longer stand to disgrace the Lord who loves them. There must be a move of the Holy Spirit upon the hearts of men so powerful and direct that they will groan with the weight of their sins and cry out in agony to be changed or die. There must be born a hatred of sin so compelling that men would rather give up life itself than do anything to dishonor the Name and the Law of God.

Put in the simplest of terms, our revivals in this day have lacked the "fire power" to truly change the hearts of men. We have been like barkers in a side show, or like candy-store merchants, offering whatever goodies might entice more people to receive Jesus. Too many have come to Jesus for what they can *get*, rather than for the love and honor due to Him who saved us from hell. Though the ineffectiveness of conversions today is not the historical cause for sin among Christians — the shallowness is itself an effect of all the other causes — nevertheless I believe true revival is the only answer — only a sufficiently powerful move of the Spirit upon the hearts of men can grant them the inner strength to bear the cost of real change! Earlier revivals carried that depth. Perhaps herein lies the greatest historical change which has resulted in born-anew Christians continuing to sin as though they had never been reborn — their conversion has never yet become that deep and real!

7

Theological and Cultural Causes for Sexual Sins

Strongholds

The greatest cultural reason for sexual sins among Christians is the power of strongholds:

> For though we live in the world, we do not wage war as the world does. The weapons we fight with are not the weapons of the world. On the contrary, *they have divine power to demolish strongholds.* We demolish arguments and every pretension that sets itself up against the knowledge of God, and we take captive every thought to make it obedient to Christ. (2 Cor. 10:3-5, NIV)

There are two kinds of strongholds. *Individual strongholds* are habitual ways of thinking which we have built within our own minds. *Corporate strongholds* are ways of thinking which come to all of us through our society and culture. Individual strongholds are unique, shaped according to each person's history and development. Corporate strongholds affect all of us, though each person at first reacts and incorporates them into his thinking in his own unique way. In the end, however, the function of corporate strongholds is to obilterate inidividual ability to respond uniquely, in order to produce a "cookie cutter" mentality amenable to control by principalities of darkness. In this chapter, I will be writing only about corporate strongholds and their effects upon all of mankind, Christians in particular.

Strongholds are practiced ways of thinking which are more than philosophies. They take hold of people's minds and rob them of the ability to think freely.

If a person builds within himself a habit, that practice (Col. 3:9) soon develops a life of its own. For example, if a man allows a habit of rebellious resistance to authority to take root in his mind and heart, that way of reacting without thinking enslaves him and impels him to foolish statements or actions, for example, when his boss gives him an order. If he decides he doesn't want that habit any longer, he finds that getting rid of it isn't so easy. The next time his boss gives him an order which seems unfair, before he can stop himself, that practice has thrown him again into saying or doing something he wishes he hadn't. Habits have a life of their own; they don't want to change or die.

Just as we can build habit structures within ourselves individually, we can build habitual societal ways of thinking. We may call them "mind sets," "traditions," "philosophies," "archetypes" or the biblical word, "strongholds," but whatever we call them, the point is that, like habits, they have a life of their own and do not want to relinquish their hold on us. "See to it that no one takes you captive through philosophy and empty deception, according to the tradition of men, according to the elementary principles of the world, rather than according to Christ" (Col. 2:8).

We are corporate creatures. "And if one member suffers, all the members suffer with it; if one member is honored, all the members rejoice with it" (1 Cor. 12: 26). It is not merely that our emotions have an impact on others. We affect one another's thoughts. Empathetically, habitual ways of thinking in our society either bless or defile us.

Strongholds rob individuals of their free will. A stronghold is like an octopus in the sea of human thought, waiting to clamp its tentacles about any unwary person whose wayward thoughts allow it to take hold. Strongholds create tunnel vision, blocking out whatever thoughts inspired by God's Word might contradict them. They cause logic to run in tight little circles, strengthening the grip of delusion.

Christian ways of thinking set men free. The Holy Spirit flows through the minds of Christians when their thinking is in accord with the Lord Jesus Christ and the Word of God: "Now the Lord is the Spirit; and where the Spirit of the Lord is, there is liberty" (2 Cor. 3:17). But when we think contrary to God's Word, flesh operates in a way that seduces and imprisons us.

Before the Second World War, Adolf Hitler began to preach to the German people that they were "the superior race." Racial superiority, with its attendant bias and hatred, is a stronghold built through centuries in the minds of mankind — Jews over Samaritans, Samaritans over Jews, Caucasians over Orientals, Africans, Indians, etc.

That stronghold established itself over the German mentality, flooding their minds with false facts and spurious logic. Whoever was not securely grounded in our Lord Jesus Christ found himself thinking thoughts of racial superiority — and many blindly followed Hitler's demagoguery into subhuman actions! Thus the "world forces of this darkness... the spiritual forces of wickedness in the heavenly places" (Eph. 6:12) used the stronghold of racial hatred to create the Holocaust!

A friend of mine was raised in the same part of the country I was. Neither of our parents was biased and they taught us to love and respect men of all races — my mother especially, since her heritage is partly from the Osage Indian tribe. But my friend moved to a southern state. Not all who live there are overcome by racial strongholds, but some people among whom he lived were. Now, my friend can hardly wait to tell me the latest "nigger" joke, apparently unaware how that grinds against the Lord's love for all men. I often hear that stronghold in his statements, and I grieve to see the freedom of his mind dissolving more and more under the influence of that mind-set.

Today's "skinheads" are expressions of the stronghold of racial hatred. These poor, benighted souls are ruled by hate and confusion, and their minds are totally captive. They have become puppets of "the world rulers of this present darkness" (vs 12, RSV), serving nought but Satan's ends as they strut their inanities before the world.

Hitler also proclaimed the "divine" right of the German Third Reich to attack other nations to establish its "ordained reign over the world." That enabled the ancient stronghold of war and aggression to gain hold of the German mind. Whoever was not sufficiently strong in Jesus found himself not only agreeing but spouting the same nonsense. And so, with very few dissenters (who were imprisoned or executed), the German nation goose-stepped off to war — and to defeat and humiliation!

Strongholds are wielded by demonic principalities: "For our struggle is not against flesh and blood, but against the rulers, against the powers, against the world forces of this darkness, against the spiritual forces of wickedness in the heavenly places" (Eph. 6:12). It is by clamping strongholds over the minds of unwary people that "world forces of this darkness" control masses of people in the world and seduce even some born-anew Christians to do their will.

The existence and operation of strongholds is unknown to most Christians. Truly, "My people are destroyed for lack of knowledge" (Hos. 4:6). Look at what the stronghold of homosexuality has enabled Satan to accomplish! Hundreds of thousands of sick, miserable, "gay" people march under its banner, their thinking impossibly warped. Coupled with the stronghold of the "rights" movement, they contribute thousands of dollars thinking they are lobbying for protection, but in many instances they are working for concessions which can do nothing but hasten their own death and possibly ours as well, spiritually, and physically, due to AIDS.

Rights movements such as that led by Martin Luther King have accomplished wonders. We need always to continue the fight for true rights. But Satan, as usual, has his counterfeit. We see the stronghold of the rights movement being manipulated every day to control our lawmakers, courts, media, etc. The strongholds of homosexuality and "rights" so pollute the minds of nearly everyone that even Christians who know it is wrong do not want to speak out for fear of being thought judgmental! Satanic world rulers wield those strongholds so as to destroy the many thousands who fall under their sway (John 10:10).

Even greater is the stronghold of sexual immorality — which employs countless tools of deception: pornography; voyeurism; "free speech," confusing the minds of legislators and judges until laws no longer uphold proper censorship and people have no protection from all kinds of smut (again, there is a right struggle for free speech, for example, to be allowed to pray in schools). Whenever a person begins to enter into spiritual adultery, or merely to fantasize about what it might be like to try a little forbidden sex, he has instant "help." If a Christian decides, "Well, I'll just watch one X-rated movie — to see what's really so sinful about it," the powers of darkness commence to warp his mind and emotions through long-established strongholds. His foolish dabbling has given them access. If he does not quickly repent, or friends do not soon get involved, "snatching [him] from the fire, . . . hating even the garment polluted by the flesh" (Jude 23), he is apt to fall quickly under the sway of the stronghold of immorality and be lost to Christ.

Strongholds are one of the greatest of all causes for sexual sins among Christians! Any concerned pastor or Christian counselor can testify to the constant grief of watching beloved friends lose their grip on reality, sailing off into delusions and sexual sins. Through lust, demonic principalities feed sexual fantasies, deceptions, excuses and justifications into Christians' minds. They pour in illicit passions and wrong desires and seek to block out the warnings of conscience. They manage to bring people who can evangelize for Satan's way: "For speaking out arrogant words of vanity they entice by fleshly desires, by sensuality, those who barely escape from the ones who live in error, promising them freedom while they themselves are slaves of corruption; for by what a man is overcome, by this he is enslaved" (2 Pet. 2:18-19).

When couples start thinking about getting separated or divorced, powers of darkness lock onto them tremendous strongholds of confusion and delusion. Haven't all of us noticed that one day we can reason with our friends; they can hear and think rightly — and the next day there is no longer any reasoning with them?!

They parrot all the usual stock phrases: "I've only got one life to live." "God doesn't want me to be unhappy for the rest of my days." "We're fighting so much. Our children would be better off if we just parted company." "We were so young when we got married." "Well, I'm just not being a very good parent. I'm sure if I divorced my wife, she could find a better father for my kids than I have been." They have lost the ability to think in ways which would contradict those lies: "Counseling would turn all that around to glory." "Your children need you, not someone else." "You haven't worked at all the options." "You have a responsibility to those children to try." To say nothing of the vows they made: ". . . for better for worse, for richer for poorer, in sickness and in health, till death us do part." The rulers of this darkness fight to keep people from remembering their marriage covenants.

Satan has poured a flood out of his mouth to sweep away "the woman," if possible (Rev.12:15). The woman is the Church. Whoever understands strongholds, and how "world rulers" wield them, can see where the spiritual warfare is for the control of men's minds. Whenever a people turns from God, as nation after nation has done in our time, God gives them up to a base mind to do those things which are degrading and despicable (Rom. 1: 21-32). God knows full well those people will be abandoned to demonic strongholds of immorality — but in His wisdom He also knows that mankind must become disgusted enough to come to true repentance! He realizes the powers of darkness are so foolish they will overplay their hand and thus cause mankind to repent. But because God also knows that the powers can so entrap men's minds that they will not be able to come to repentance unaided, *His plan depends on Christians answering His call to intercede. Christians must stand in the gap and war against the strongholds on people's minds, praying for strength in their spirits so that men can come to the repentance God has wanted all along.*

That is the importance of this chapter. God's people must learn how and where to go into battle. Zeal without knowledge often plunges men and women into warfare God didn't call for. Fools rush in where angels fear to tread. Warriors get hurt and lost to the cause that way.

When Paula and I learned about strongholds, and how to defeat them, we characteristically leaped into the fray to deliver all mankind! We were going to get those things off every person in the Lord's Church and in the world, right now! Two things happened: first, we wore ourselves out! In a few days, we couldn't put one foot in front of another! So we said our usual fervent and highly intellectual prayer — "Help!" And the Lord patiently taught us to wait upon Him and to tackle only those problems He was anointing us for in that moment. The second was that people got worse! We had forgotten that casting away principalities and strongholds is much like casting out demons: if the person is not ready to repent and change, the result will be seven times as bad!

The Antidote

1) *Listen to the Lord.* Be like sergeants, who get the battle plan the day before the battle. Tackle whatever principalities and strongholds He says to defeat — when, how and where He says. Name the stronghold. Bind its power under the anointing of the Spirit, not in the misbegotten zeal of the flesh.

2) *Comprehend the strategy of warfare against strongholds and principalities.* Don't go off half-cocked. Strongholds are not themselves demonic entities. They are habitual structures of thinking and feeling in the flesh, wielded

by ruling demons. You don't cast flesh out. Flesh is to be taken to the cross by repentance, confession and prayer. The principality must be bound and cast away, but not the stronghold. Bind the power of the stronghold. Command it to be still. But leave it there. Its effect in the person will be transformed by grace to become part of his compassion and strength in ministry.

Remember also that once you start into battle against principalities, you can't stop when you want to. The battle is something like being pregnant — you can't quit just because you get tired of it! You will have to persevere until the one in sin comes to repentance. The purpose of the warfare is to restore the others to ability to think straight and to stand on his own. You are battling against principalities, reclaiming the victory Jesus has already won, in order to break their grip upon the stronghold and the person so that he can come to himself and say as did the prodigal, "I will get up and go to my father" (Luke 15:18).

When you have won for him the freedom to think again, there is no guarantee that the person will choose rightly. This means: first, you must pray for him to have strength in his spirit in order to come to a good repentance. It takes strength of spirit to admit fault and ask for forgiveness. Second, you may have to pray daily for a long time. Your prayers are purchasing time and the capability to repent. But the very thing you are fighting for is his freedom to think for himself, so you cannot make him choose rightly.

Therefore, never fight the battle alone. In the first place, it's too dangerous. The powers of darkness will move upon whatever weakness you have until you have neither time nor energy for warfare: "No soldier in active service entangles himself in the affairs of everyday life, so that he may please the one who enlisted him as a soldier" (2 Tim. 2:4). Satan's soldiers, like their master, know the Word and therefore want to entangle the Lord's warriors in many difficulties until they become ineffective. Keep your agenda as clear as possible when battling strongholds and powers of darkness.

In the second place:
> Two are better than one because they have a good return for their labor. For if either of them falls, the one will lift up his companion. But woe to the one who falls when there is not another to lift him up. Furthermore, if two lie down together they keep warm, but how can one be warm alone? And if one can overpower him who is alone, two can resist him. A cord of three strands is not quickly torn apart. (Eccles. 4: 9-12)

Two or more can keep vigil, so that one rests while another carries the banner. Several can compare visions and insights and check each other, whereas one alone can be carried away into delusions (Eph. 4:14). Satan's favorite trick is what might be called a "war of attrition." He simply wears us out with trivial matters, until we are too weary to bring the victory to full conclusion. But when several are joined in warfare, he is not so able to wear everyone out. "And let us not lose heart in doing good, for *in due time we shall reap if we do not grow weary*" (Gal. 6:9).

3) *Teaching must complete the victory.* Once deliverance has been achieved and repentance has set the person free, there must be careful teaching so he doesn't happen into the same pitfalls again. The person must come to understand what entrapped him and how, lest he think he can dabble again in whatever it was with impunity.

We do not have to stand helplessly by while our friends fall prey to the strongholds of deception rampant in our culture today. We are called to spiritual warfare as never before:

> Let the godly ones exult in glory;
> Let them sing for joy on their beds.
> Let the high praises of God be in their mouth,
> And a two-edged sword in their hand.

To execute vengeance on the nations [i.e. demons]
And punishments on the peoples; [fallen angels]
To bind their kings with chains, [principalities]
And their nobles with fetters of iron; [rulers]
To execute on them the judgment written;
This is an honor for all His godly ones.
Praise the Lord! (Ps. 149:5-9)

The warfare against strongholds and principalities is not for a select few. It is for every Christian. All of us are called to stand in warfare, proclaiming what Jesus Christ has already accomplished (Matt. 28:18; Phil. 2:9-11). I long for the day when we shall let go our petty concerns and stand, ". . . an exceedingly great army" (Ezek. 37:10).

The Stronghold of Theological Confusion

The greatest and most deceptively confusing stronghold in our culture, one which has so far successfully resisted spiritual warfare, is a way of thinking about ourselves as bodies and spirits.

There are two ways of thinking about ourselves as bodies, souls and spirits. Both are theological. Both affect us, whether or not we know of them. They are part of our culture and thus become part of our thinking. We make decisions and act on the basis of them, without ever having known of them or having consciously thought them through. One is Christian. The other is of the antichrist. Unfortunately, most of the world (including many Christians) usually operate on the basis of the antichrist way, thinking their way is good and acceptable.

Both ways of thinking spring from ancient roots. Both were being formed well before the time of our Lord's life and death. Both are so rooted in customs and practices that every one of us is affected by them subconsciously, unless one understands and breaks the hold of antichrist thinking on his heart and mind.

The antichrist way of thinking says that man and the whole universe are a dichotomy: matter and spirit are totally separate and war against each other. It states that spirit is good but matter is defiled. Spirit, for the most part, is high up in the heavens, whereas matter is down below, fallen and defiled.

As we will see, this wrong way of thinking about ourselves as bodies and spirits lies behind countless adulteries and fornications. It causes men to think that pornography and voyeurism are not harmful. It makes prostitution profitable. It lies behind the destruction of moral barriers which has permitted R-and X-rated movies.

Amazingly, most Christian schools and colleges, even many seminaries, are unaware that this way of thinking is wrong and therefore espouse it as though it were Christian, "TEACHING AS DOCTRINES THE PRECEPTS OF MEN" (Matt. 15:9b and Mark. 7:7).

In some Christians, this erroneous theology misconstrues the Bible's use of the word "flesh" to make it mean that the human body is itself evil and must be mortified. Orthodox interpretation of Scripture says that when the Word speaks of "flesh," it usually is referring to the world's ways which have become a "body" of ways of thinking and acting in opposition to our Lord.

St. Paul says, "Wretched man that I am! Who will set me free from the body of this death?" (Rom. 7:24), and ". . . if by the Spirit you are putting to death the deeds of the body, you will live" (Rom. 8:13). Orthodox teaching says that he is not speaking of the physical body but of the "body" of sinful practices within his nature. Else he could not say elsewhere that ". . . you are a temple of God, and that the Spirit of God dwells in you . . ." (1 Cor. 3:16). The Holy Spirit will not dwell in an unclean vessel. Our body is clean and good. But those controlled by the antichrist mind-set believe that the physical body is itself evil. As we will see, that misconception lies behind much of the sexual sinning of born-anew Christians.

All around Palestine and throughout the known

world at the time of our Lord's birth, the culture was dominated by the antichrist way of thinking. It had its basis in Hindu philosophy and theology, which holds that pure spirit is utterly transcendent, separated from anything on earth. Spirit is good. Matter, or flesh, is bad. Mankind has fallen from being pure spirit into incarnation in the body. It is bad to be in the body. One must progress through the wheels of Samsara (cycles of transmigration, or successive incarnations in animal and human form) and Karma (the sum of a person's actions in one incarnation which determines his next incarnation, thus similar to the law of sowing and reaping but involving also fate, or "kismet," and the necessity to experience these various stages in order to be purified for Nirvana — their concept of the final heaven).

The hope is to become pure spirit once more and never again have to be reincarnated again. Thus if one is good, and resigned to his fate in this life, he may be reincarnated in the next life in a higher caste, and so progress to become a Brahmin (the highest caste) and finally escape from the cycles of rebirth altogether. In this belief system, one does not want to do too much to help another lest he disturb that person's Karma and so cause the other to have to relive the situation in another reincarnation to accomplish what your intervention prevented.

This theology is exactly opposite to Christian doctrine! Matter and earthly things are not bad; God's Spirit flows in and through all things (Eph. 4:6). We do not want to escape from the body in order to become pure spirit but rather, we want to be perfected within it or, failing that, to be resurrected within the body. We do not want to be resigned to whatever comes upon us but to redeem all of mankind and all of history for our Lord.

From this, let me sound the warning to those who think they can borrow from Eastern religions: mantras and chakras (Hindu techniques for chanting, praying, meditating) have behind them vast strongholds of deception. Hindu meditation creates passivity, which leads to control by principalities wielding strongholds. Christian meditation involves active encounter as we meet and commune with our living Lord; it is in no way similar to Eastern meditation. We do not need, nor will we be helped by borrowing, techniques from that, or any other religion.

Yoga and similar exercise techniques developed to aid the body have behind them huge strongholds of Eastern philosophy. So do the martial arts. Christians can, and have, developed exercises and routines which do not invite strongholds and principalities of deception. Many policemen and policewomen today receive some training in Eastern martial arts. I do not know whether martial techniques can be divorced from their base. Many informed Christians deny that possibility. Knowing the power of strongholds, I fear they may be right.

When Adam and Eve fell, they (and thus we) lost the ability to commune closely with God. Adam and Eve's spirits before the Fall were perfectly in tune with the Lord's. When He walked and talked with them in the cool of the day, they "read" His Spirit. They understood His moods and comprehended His thoughts with perfect trust and no fear at all. But sin shattered that ability to read His Spirit and understand His thoughts. Satan's defilement replaced intimacy with fear and untrust. What followed was devolution, until whenever God approached the sons and daughters of earth, they could grasp only an iota of what He wanted to communicate.

Of course, He could have used His power to force them to understand Him rightly, but then they would have become robots and not sons and daughters with whom He could fellowship throughout eternity. From God's point of view, the question was: How do I restore mankind to the capacity to have fellowship with Me without violating their free will?"

Satan did not surprise God with something that forced Him to change His eternal plans. In His wisdom, He foreknew exactly what Satan and Adam and Eve would do. From His ground plan, before creation, He had mapped out the way back.

Wherever our Lord has approached a people, they have caught a piece of the vision of His nature, but only a piece. He came to men in India, and they caught the idea that God is a trinity — but one of the three was named Shiva, the destroyer! And they thought life in the body was a curse, rather than being a gift and the gateway to heaven. He came to men in China, and they received the idea that He is Wisdom — and missed nearly everything else. In the isthmus of America and in Hawaii, when He approached, they foretyped the blood sacrifice of His Son — and murdered thousands in orgies of sacrificial rites! And so it went. Nobody knew Him for who and what He really is.

But God had known that would happen, and was preparing men to receive a fuller and more accurate revelation of himself — indeed, the fulness of revelation in our Lord Jesus Christ.

When the time was ripe, He spoke to a man called Abram. Through him and his descendants, God would begin to reveal His true nature. He made a bargain with them. He would send them into 400 years of captivity, and then He would bring them out into a land flowing with milk and honey (Gen. 15:13-21). If they would be His people and show to the world what His nature is, then He would be their God and bless them in the land.

God knew they would fail. But He also knew that Israel would prepare the ground in the hearts and minds of His people for the coming of His Son, through whom once for all He would reveal who He is and what He is like.

But, the revelation of God's nature in our Lord Jesus Christ came to a Hebrew people who were surrounded by ancient strongholds of thought which threatened from the very outset to undo the purity of the revelation, if not to destroy it altogether!

The Babylonian story of creation said that the god Marduk stuffed the four winds of heaven into his mother Tiamat's mouth, whereupon her belly distended, she died of gas poisoning and fell to the ground. Marduk took his knife and slit her belly. He lifted the top part, which became the heavens. The blood and guts running out at the bottom became the earth! With that story of creation, could one respect the earth and cherish one's own body?!

The Egyptian story proclaimed that there had been a mud flood, in which mud hillocks arose. On one of the hills a man stood. One version says he spat; the other that he masturbated. The spittle or the semen is creation! That's what formed the earth. That's what we were formed from. With such a story, could mankind rejoice in its existence?!

Contrast that to the biblical story: a good and holy God said, " 'Let there be light'; and there was light. And God saw that the light was good..." (Gen. 1:3-4a). For six days that holy and loving God did His work of creation, and every day He saw that it was good. On the sixth day, God took that good, clean dust of the earth, formed man and breathed His own holy breath into him and man became a living soul (2:7). And when God had created man and woman, "... God saw all that He had made, and behold, it was very good" (1:31a). What a difference!

But that revelation came to a people immersed in a culture dominated and controlled by strongholds of deception. Three centuries before the birth of Jesus, Alexander the Great had conquered Palestine and the entire middle-eastern region. That began the Hellenistic period, in which Greek thought, ways and language were dominant. Aristotelian philosophy pervaded the mentality of the time. Later, the *Pax Romana* of the Roman Empire afforded an atmosphere in which Greek culture and ways of thinking could flourish. Indeed, the New Testament was written in *Koine* (a Greek dialect common throughout Roman dominions at the time and somewhat comparable to today's American English).

Greek mentality of the day held to a dualistic view of nature akin to the Hindu — spirit is good flesh is bad — and so was scandalized when asked to believe that

Jesus, the very Son of God, was born as a lowly human being, amid all that pain and blood. That He would be suckled at the breast and have his diapers changed — horrors! So a number of Hellenistic heresies were spawned:

A man named Cerinthus came up with the heresy called "adoptionism." God Himself in Jesus could not have been born through the defilement of a human womb, so God just found a grown man and zapped him (adopted him) with His own Spirit!

Since it was unthinkable that God would become flesh (John 1:14), another heresy held that He just appeared to have a body, floated around a while, and then went back up to become pure spirit again. That heresy was called "Docetism," from the Greek word *docein* meaning "to appear." As we will see, though the Church branded that as heresy and rejected it theologically, it continued to flourish as a stronghold. Docetism is the most besetting, defiling stronghold afflicting all Christendom today.

It was repellent to Greeks, who thought that when Socrates drank the poisoned hemlock he would thereby escape the defilements of physicality, to be asked to embrace a faith that celebrated being raised again in a physical body! The very purpose of dying was to flee the body! Therefore St. Paul had to write to the Corinthians (Greeks) to say that Jesus had indeed been raised in a real physical body, and we will be also (1 Cor. 15).

Greek Gnostics (from *gnosis*, or knowledge — in short, men who believed that they would be saved by right thinking rather than by the person of the Savior, our Lord Jesus Christ) held that the world was created by a demiurge (a being, lesser than the supreme god) whose mixed-up ways botched and defiled the earth. Thus, of course, matter and the body were tinged with evil. It was against this heresy that the opening words of John's gospel fairly thunder with truth:

In the beginning was the Word, and the

Word was with God, and the Word was God.
[No demiurge, no half-god, but God himself.]
He was in the beginning with God.
[Gnostic theology had said that the lesser god was created as an afterthought by the supreme god.]
All things came into being by Him, and apart from Him nothing came into being that has come into being.
[Gnostics had said that the supreme god had created some things rightly, but the demiurge had added some mistaken things which had defiled the supreme god's work.]
In Him was life, and the life was the light of men.
[Gnostics believed that the lesser god had in him some darkness, which had brought death and confusion to mankind.] (John 1:1-4)

Having established that Jesus is no lesser, mistaken god, John went on to demolish the Docetic idea that He didn't really incarnate and thus only floated around a while looking like He had a body: "And the Word became flesh, and dwelt among us, and we beheld His glory, glory as of the only begotten from the Father, full of grace and truth" (1:14). Jesus did not merely visit flesh, like water in a jar. He became flesh. Nor did He lose any of His divinity in the transition; He was full of grace and truth.

Thus the apostles encountered the strongholds of Gnosticism and Docetism and destroyed them as a theology. But the strongholds are tenacious. They keep returning, century after century. Nearly three hundred years later, at the Council of Nicaea in 325 A.D., the battle lines were drawn again. Docetic Gnosticism, through Arianism, tried to maintain that Jesus was of like but not the same nature as God. The debate was fought over one little letter, iota. Would the statement of faith say homo-ousios or homoi-ousios? The first meant "of the same identical nature," the second "of like but not the same nature" (The Gnostics' demiurge all over again.)

Against the Arians stood Athanasius, a great ascetic hermit and theologian, insisting that Jesus was of the same nature as the Father. Athanasius won and the deposit of faith was saved from error. Therefore the Nicene Creed proclaims so resoundingly: ". . .God of gods, light of light, very God of very God; begotten, not made, being of one substance with the Father, by whom all things were made. . ."

The stronghold as a theology had been defeated again, but it persists, recurring here and there to this day, mainly through Aristotelian thought (which accepted the basic world-view of Eastern mentality). That philosophy became the prevailing philosophy, not only of that age but up to the present. Its basic tenets (that all things are controlled by cause and effect, and that anything which does not breathe has no spirit in it) came into Christian theology almost unchallenged. With those seemingly innocuous concepts came the belief that spirit is good and matter is bad. Sliding into acceptance along with that was the idea that the body is evil, and therefore so is sex.

Marcion, a Gnostic theologian who wrote ca. 100 A.D., said all sex is bad and taught that all his followers should maintain complete celibacy. Though he was excommunicated as a heretic, his thoughts lived on in the stronghold of Docetism which has hung over the Church since the beginning.

Let us see how the stronghold of docetism has invaded and defiled many in the Church:

1) In the nineteenth century, which was dominated by the religious spirit of Docetism, men and women both in the Catholic and Protestant faiths were taught that sex was nasty. Catholics were taught to go to confession if they enjoyed marital sex! Mothers taught their daughters that men were nasty because they wanted sex. To be dutiful wives you had to "let them have it," and of course it was necessary for procreation, but if you enjoyed it, you were being sinful!

2) Many men and women were taught that the body is sinful and that a true Christian will mortify its desires.

All passions were thought to be of the devil. A true Christian would not let them live. Paintings of Jesus depicted a baby-faced, idealistic, less-than-human young man, who was of course too pure and innocent to have any real feelings.

3) A mother would be horrified and ashamed if she found her children had discovered their "private parts" and fondled them. She would berate the children and make sure their Papa took them to the wood shed for a little "razor strap education."

4) Women's clothing had to cover everything, from throat to ankles, even well into the twentieth century. I can remember a hired hand on the ranch in Oklahoma who was mortified and embarrassed because he happened to glimpse my mother's ankle as he helped her onto the saddle of her horse! Bodies were not to be seen! At all!

Turn-of-the-century bathing suits covered so much, one wonders how anybody could have swum in them. It may be that part of the reason some of our modern bathing suits reveal so much is out of reaction and rebellion against the foolish Docetic prudery of those days. An extreme example (during the Victorian era) had housewives sewing pantaloons to cover the "limbs" on the piano! (One didn't refer to them as "legs" —that would have been too brazen.) Paula's great-grandmother bore nine children and boasted till her dying day that her husband had never seen her naked!

5) Several times in the first two churches I pastored, women got up and marched out of the service, incensed that I had mentioned sex from the pulpit, of all the nerve! What I actually had said was merely an innocuous reference to another subject. These women thought they were being righteous Christians. In actual fact, their minds had been sullied by antichrist strongholds of deception.

Now let us see what effects Docetic strongholds have had upon morality:

1) Some denominations, teaching that the body is evil, created feelings of guiltiness and shame whenever

their members engaged in marital sex, especially if they enjoyed it. That produced unhealthy suppressions of natural and normal feelings, which in turn inhibited learning how to please one another and, furthermore, squelched God-ordained regularity in sexual activity:

> Let the husband fulfill his duty to his wife, and likewise also the wife to her husband. The wife does not have authority over her own body, but the husband does; and likewise also the husband does not have authority over his own body, but the wife does. Stop depriving one another, except by agreement for a time that you may devote yourselves to prayer, and come together again lest Satan tempt you because of your lack of self-control. (1 Cor. 7:3-5)

Though couples may try to suppress natural passions in the act of love play, those passions are cannot be turned off. If denied, they will surface in unwanted places. During the Victorian age, which was ruled by Docetic strongholds, it was common for men to have mistresses. They had sex with their wives to produce heirs but would not allow their passions in marital embraces. I remember hearing of a man who, totally embarrassed, apologized profusely to his wife because he had been so crass and unthinking as to have aroused her sexual passions the night before! But with their mistresses, since sin was already involved, men could give full vent to their passions. They enjoyed sex with their mistresses — and endured it at home!

Today, in those denominations whose theology says that the body is sinful, I have ministered to more cases of adultery by far than in any other group! Recently I was visiting with several other leaders in the ministry of Christian counseling and heard them state exactly the same! Faulty theology leaves believers in those denominations vulnerable both to the dynamic of suppression and expression and to the stronghold of immoral sex.

2) Pornography and voyeurism thrive wherever sex is believed to be unclean. The natural curiosity of children is made to seem nasty and evil. That provokes rebellious desire to see what is forbidden. It is the sense that the viewer is getting away with some childish forbidden thing that gives pornography and voyeurism the power to allure.

In one church I served, many of the members belonged to a local men's club. They decided to hold a stag party. Strippers came and began to walk among them in various stages of undress. Our next-door neighbor, a medical doctor, left the room and was sitting at the bar having a drink by himself. One of the church members came out and said, "Hey Doc, you oughta come in and take a look at this! You've never seen anything like it!" Doc merely responded, "You wanta bet?!" Voyeurism held no fascination for him who examined naked bodies every day! Its power lay in the childish naughtiness of it.

If Christians thought in Hebraic-Christian terms, they would realize that the body is holy and clean and good. Therefore we do not defile it. But they have been taught to think in dichotomous terms: "That's just a body over there, and what I do with that body has nothing to do with the rest of me."

I have counseled husbands who committed adultery and then said to their wives, "But honey, that didn't mean anything to me. That was only physical. You're the one I really love." They did not know that there is no such thing as sex which is only physical. Their minds were seduced by the stronghold of Docetism. "Or do you not know that the one who joins himself to a harlot is one body with her? For He says, 'THE TWO WILL BECOME ONE FLESH' " (1 Cor. 6:16). Had those husbands thought in Hebraic-Christian terms, they would have known that they could not enter into sex with anyone merely body-to-body. Prostitution thrives because men and women think they can enjoy physical sex without being involved in any other way. That is Docetic heresy.

One of the most cogent reasons sexual sin is rampant among

Christians today is that Satan has sold them the lie that what they do with their body bears little relation to what their spirit is and does. Solely by the grace of God I have remained true to Paula, but part of the way that grace has worked has been through His teaching me early on that only Paula has been anointed by Him to touch me in sexual ways. There is no way I could ever sexually touch any woman only physically. Any woman other than Paula would tell my soul lies about myself. Only she is joined to me by God to complete me and tell me who I am.

If Christians thought as Hebraic-Christians, they would shun immorality violently: "Flee immorality. Every other sin that a man commits is outside the body, but the immoral man sins against his own body. Or do you not know that your body is a temple of the Holy Spirit who is in you, whom you have from God, and that you are not your own?" (1 Cor. 6:18-19).

If we thought as Hebraic-Christians, we could not tolerate pornography and voyeurism. Knowing that every Christian is a temple of God's spirit, we could not stand to defile it: "For you have been bought with a price: therefore glorify God in your body" (1 Cor. 6:20). ". . . but I say to you, that everyone who looks on a woman. . ." (Matt. 5:28).

Because of the stronghold of Docetism, confusion reigns in men's hearts and minds in the commonest daily acts . A man sits down to eat. He says a grace — that's being spiritual. Eating, he thinks, is only physical. He goes to work; that's physical. The grace at supper is spiritual, but eating is again physical. Maybe his wife says a prayer with him before bedtime — spiritual. Then he wants to make love to his wife — and thinks that's something only physical. All that is deception! Since God's Spirit lives within him, everything he does is both physical and spiritual. No Christian can compartmentalize life like that — but he thinks he can because of the stronghold of Docetism.

Thus he questions, as so many Christians have asked me, "But what can I do at work that is specifically

Christian?" That he asks at all is evidence of his mind's delusion. Whatever he does, wherever he may be, is Christian. He does not understand that all of life is sacramental, that there is no separation for Christians between what is "secular" and what is "Christian" or "spiritual." If he were imbued with the sense that whatever he does manifests the life of our Lord Jesus on earth, would that not serve as a check on his actions? But he thinks that life in the world and life in Christ are two separate entities. Immorality thus becomes something we want to confess to the priest so we'll make it to Heaven (in case it happens to exist), but we don't really see how physical sinning has anything to do with our spiritual life in Christ. To those in deception the two are separate.

Think on these things. The only antidote to the stronghold of Docetism in the life of the Church today is for enough Christians to see it clearly, to hate it and its effects in Christians' lives, and to teach and pray it away.

8

Contemporary Theological Imbalances That Cause Sexual and Other Sins

Cheap Grace

I believe that one of the greatest theological reasons born-anew Christians have become callous and careless about sin in these days is that we have fallen into a delusion many call "cheap grace." It is not merely that we have rightly preached the grace and forgiveness of the Lord Jesus Christ and wrongly tended to overlook His severity in judgment. Imbalance in presenting the gospel may induce some to think they can do anything and Jesus will simply wash it away. But I believe there is a greater error involved, far more damaging to Christian morality.

The delusion is that forgiveness does away with any and all of the after-effects of sin, that there will be no further results from sin once Jesus has forgiven us, and moreover, that forgiveness does away with the necessity for discipline. When Christians swallow that deception, they are tempted to think that they can do anything with impunity because Jesus will take care of it and that will be the end of it. That is what we mean by "cheap grace."

Cheap grace is neither the gospel of good news nor justifiable in the Scriptures. Somehow we have gotten the false idea that we can commit any sort of heinous sin, and once we have said the magic words, "Forgive me," nothing else of harm or discipline should follow! That is a horrible delusion, especially regarding sexual sins among believers. If a man falls into adultery, he has demeaned the glory of his brother (1 Thess. 4:6). There will be destruction and loss, no matter how full his repentance nor how complete his forgiveness and restoration!

Part of the tragedy is that a portion of the splendor of that man's ministry is gone forever. He may continue to serve, even perhaps quite successfully. But his chasteness before the Lord is lost. It can never be regained.

But discipline will also fall. We have been amazed to see how often some sort of curse settles on such men's lives, which no exorcist and no amount of prayer can lift. Most commonly, their finances are constantly in trouble from then on. Saddest of all, too often we see tragedy striking the lives of their children! Remember what happened to King David when he committed adultery with Bathsheba? Though he himself was forgiven, discipline fell through the death of his child: "Then the Lord struck the child that Uriah's widow bore to David..." (2 Sam. 12:15ff). *Deaths and tragedies stalk the families of those who fall into adultery!*

Someone might ask, "How can I love a God who would strike my child for the sins I have done? How can that be fair?" At least two confusions are at work here. First, we fail in this day to comprehend the corporateness of the life we live in Christ. The fact that God struck David's child does not mean that He wanted to.

The Scripture speaks in a personal mode when addressing legal matters of reaping. "God struck..." means that the law of sowing and reaping was fulfilled upon David's child. How is that fair? All the advances in medicine we enjoy today, which save our lives and bless us with health and joy, are gifts we reap unearned from the labors of our forefathers. Likewise all the technology which dresses us, warms our houses, drives our cars, and gives us the sometimes dubious blessings of television is inherited from our ancestors — totally undeserved by us. Shall we say that it is fair for us to reap the blessings of our ancestors but unfair if we reap the evils they have sown? Thus our children suffer when we sin. God is more grieved than we are when that kind of harm happens.

The second confusion has to with punishment or vindictiveness. It may look to some as though God had to take it out on somebody, so He picked on that poor, innocent child of David! Or on some modern-day children suffering after their parents have fallen into various sins. "There is no fear in love; but perfect love casts out fear, because fear involves punishment, and the one who fears is not perfected in love" (1 John 4:18). God is not vindictive. We project onto God our unhealed resentments of authority figures who punished us, perhaps too hurtfully and abusively. Whoever is "perfected in love" has come to see the true source of his confusions and fears and is freed by the power of the cross to see God as He really is — pure and kindly Love without limit for all of us.

We have not wanted to realize that the sins we commit drastically affect our children. Several times I have quoted from Hosea 4:6, "My people are destroyed for lack of knowledge." Listen to the last part of that verse: "Because you have rejected knowledge, I also will reject you from being My priest. Since you have forgotten the law of your God, I also will forget your children."

The Apocrypha is not regarded by most of the Church as canonical; I quote the following not as Scripture, but as evidence of the way the people of Bible times thought about sin and its effects:

> For the fruit of good labors is renowned, and the root of understanding does not fail. But children of adulterers will not come to maturity, and the offspring of an unlawful union will perish. Even if they live long they will be held of no account, and finally their old age will be without honor. If they die young, they will have no hope and no consolation in the day of decision. For the end of an unrighteous generation is grievous.
>
> (Wisdom of Solomon 3:16-19)

> For mercy and wrath are with the Lord; He
> is mighty to forgive, and He pours out wrath.
> As great is his mercy, so great also is His reproof;
> he judges a man according to his deeds. The
> sinner will not escape with his plunder, and the
> patience of the godly will not be frustrated.
> (Ecclesiasticus 16:11b-13)

Deuteronomy 23:2 says it even more starkly than the
Wisdom of Solomon: "No one of illegitimate birth shall
enter the assembly of the Lord; none of his descendants,
even to the tenth generation, shall enter the assembly of
the Lord." Jesus was born to parents thought to have been
involved in fornication precisely to lift that curse from
mankind! We rightly believe He has paid the price once
for all. But the tragedy is that we have carried mercy so
far as to obliterate the discipline of God which also is His
love for us.

Wherever lack of repentance does not allow
forgiveness, the full effect of the law of sowing and reaping
descends upon our children. I think perhaps all of us have
seen instances in which, though parents have said they
repented and have received absolution for their sins,
terrible things have still fallen upon their childrens' lives!
One can only wonder: was their repentance not full
enough so that they reaped the Law anyway? Wherever
fulness of repentance allows, the cross of Christ fulfils the
legal necessity for reaping. The impersonal law of
Galatians 6:7 is personally satisfied by the atonement of
Jesus on the cross.

But God's mercy does not do away with discipline.
His discipline will still fall upon the sinner.

I know the Body does not want to hear this. We have
too long believed in cheap grace. But it is actually very
simple. When I was a child, my father would catch me
in some sin, and then he would sit me down to talk:
"Jackie, I want you to know your mother and I forgive
you, and we love you, but now I am going to have to
spank you." *Forgiveness did not mean that discipline could*

be eliminated. Rather, it meant that because they loved me, they would have to write on my heart, by the pain of discipline, what I had failed to learn the easy way.

I need to say it again, another way, so that we grasp it rightly! Somehow we have come to think that the blood of Jesus will wipe away all our sins and nothing dire ought to result once we have confessed and been forgiven! Let me repeat, brothers and sisters, that is a terrible mistake and delusion!! The blood does wash away our guilt, and restores us to fellowship and eventually to heaven; but it does not stay the disciplining hand of God! Remember that we are discussing the adulteries of born-anew Christians.

Some time ago, I was praising God for His gentleness and His kindness. Suddenly, His presence was powerfully upon me, and He said rather sternly, "You love your picture of Me!" I knew a thousand things in that moment of confrontation! Among which was I was allowing Him to show me only a small part of who He really is. From that day on, He began to take me on an Emmaus walk, opening my eyes to many sides of His nature that we in our modern snugness will not allow ourselves to see. Particularly, He began to reveal to me the glory of His love for us in sternness and discipline, and to let me know that one of the major reasons Christians sin so flagrantly today is that they do not know Him for who He really is.

The tragedy is that today's Christians do not understand the blessing of discipline:

> . . .you have forgotten the exhortation which is addressed to you as sons,"MY SON, DO NOT REGARD LIGHTLY THE DISCIPLINE OF THE LORD, NOR FAINT WHEN YOU ARE REPROVED BY HIM;FOR THOSE WHOM THE LORD LOVES HE DISCIPLINES, AND HE SCOURGES EVERY SON WHOM HE RECEIVES." It is for discipline that you endure; God deals with you as with sons; for what son

is there whom his father does not discipline?

But if you are without discipline, of which all have become partakers, then you are illegitimate children and not sons.

Furthermore, we had earthly fathers to discipline us, and we respected them; shall we not much rather be subject to the Father of spirits, and live?

For they disciplined us for a short time as seemed best to them, but He disciplines us for our good, that we may share His holiness.

All discipline for the moment seems not to be joyful, but sorrowful; yet to those who have been trained by it, afterwards it yields the peaceful fruit of righteousness. (Heb. 12:5-11)

By discipline (and other loving touches) our loving heavenly Father fulfils the promise of His covenant: "I will put My law within them, and on their heart I will write it..." (Jer. 31:33b). By discipline, He prepares us for eternity.

Discipline is severe or light, depending on our degree of intention to sin when we know what is right and what is wrong: "And that slave who knew his master's will and did not get ready or act in accord with his will, shall receive many lashes, but the one who did not know it, and committed deeds worthy of a flogging, will receive but few" (Luke 12:47-48a). Note that this means Christian leaders, who know better, will receive "many lashes." And even those who do not know better will receive "a few." Why? Because God loves us, and must write on our hearts the lessons that will keep us from falling again.

Discipline is harsh or gentle, depending on the degree of pain and suffering the Lord knows is required to work His weight of glory in our hearts. (The following Scripture from Corinthians concerns that kind of suffering which comes from noble service to the Lord, but the principle of the effect of suffering remains the same.):

Therefore we do not lose heart, but though our outer man is decaying, yet our inner man is being renewed day by day. For momentary, light affliction is producing for us an eternal weight of glory far beyond all comparison, while we look not at the things which are seen, but at the things which are not seen; for the things which are seen are temporal, but the things which are not seen are eternal.

(2 Cor. 4:16-18)

Stern discipline is for him who forsakes the way;
He who hates reproof will die.

(Prov. 15:10)

Behold, how happy is the man whom God reproves,
So do not despise the discipline of the Almighty.
For He inflicts pain, and gives relief;
He wounds, and His hands also heal.

(Job 5:17-18)

To me, a greater tragedy is that too few comprehend the distinction between discipline and punishment. Discipline is applied to us personally, precisely because we are loved and forgiven. Punishment comes upon those who are not repentant, and/or whose sinning is repetitive. Punishment most often comes upon us by the impersonal reaping of the Law, which is always more harmful than personal discipline, "For they sow the wind, And they reap the whirlwind" (Hos. 8:7a). Some reap though they think they have repented, but buckets of tears are not repentance. Repentance means not only turning around but making amends.

It is pride and arrogance and an unrepentant heart which brings punishment:

Thus I will punish the world for its evil,
And the wicked for their iniquity;

I will also put an end to the arrogance of the proud, And abase the haughtiness of the ruthless. (Isa. 13:11)

Most importantly concerning the subject matter of this book, punishment is especially severe for sexual sinning persisted in without repentance:

...then the Lord knows how to rescue the godly from temptation, and to keep the unrighteous under punishment for the day of judgment, and especially those who indulge the flesh in its corrupt desires and despise authority...suffering wrong as the wages of doing wrong. They count it a pleasure to revel in the daytime. They are stains and blemishes, reveling in their deceptions, as they carouse with you, having eyes full of adultery and that never cease from sin, enticing unstable souls, having a heart trained in greed, accursed children;... For speaking out arrogant words of vanity they entice by fleshly desires, by sensuality, those who barely escape from the ones who live in error, promising them freedom while they themselves are slaves of corruption; for by what a man is overcome, by this he is enslaved. For if after they have escaped the defilements of the world by the knowledge of the Lord and Savior Jesus Christ, they are again entangled in them and are overcome, the last state has become worse for them than the first. For it would be better for them not to have known the way of righteousness, than having known it, to turn away from the holy commandment delivered to them. It has happened to them according to the true proverb, "A DOG RETURNS TO ITS VOMIT," and "A sow, after washing, returns to wallowing in the mire."

(selected verses from 2 Pet. 2:9-22)

Just as Sodom and Gomorrah and the cities around them, since they in the same way as these indulged in gross immorality and went after strange flesh, are exhibited as an example, in undergoing the punishment of eternal... (Jude 7)

The results of our ignorance concerning discipline and punishment are manifold:

1) *We remove ourselves from His Fatherhood and from the words of life:*
Cease listening, my son, to discipline,
And you will stray from the words of knowledge. (Prov. 19:27)

Whoever loves discipline loves knowledge,
But he who hates reproof is stupid. (12:1)

He who neglects discipline despises himself,
But he who listens to reproof acquires understanding. (15:32)

Like a city that is broken into and without walls
Is a man who has no control over his spirit. (25:28)

2) *When discipline comes, we fail to receive it for what it is, or appreciate it as love:*
Poverty and shame will come to him who neglects discipline,
But he who regards reproof will be honored. (13:18)

A fool rejects his father's discipline,
But he who regards reproof is prudent. (15:5)

3) *Therefore we go right on sinning, so that what would have been blessing must become punishment. His discipline would have drawn us closer to Him, but we never even knew that what was happening was His love, disciplining us:*

My son, do not reject the discipline of the Lord,
Or loathe His reproof,
For whom the Lord loves He reproves,
Even as a father, the son in whom he delights.
(3:11,12)

For the commandment is a lamp, and the teaching is light;
And reproofs for discipline are the way of life. (6:23)

4) *Most importantly, this generation has lost holy fear of God, and dread of sin. I suggest the reader devour the following passages most thoughtfully.* (Though they refer mainly to the sin of apostasy, the principle concerning sin and its results is the same for sexual or any other wilful sinning):

For in the case of those who have once been enlightened and have tasted of the heavenly gift and have been made partakers of the Holy Spirit, and have tasted the good word of God and the powers of the age to come, and then have fallen away, it is impossible to renew them again to repentance, since they again crucify to themselves the Son of God, and put Him to open shame. For ground that drinks the rain which often falls upon it and brings forth vegetation useful to those for whose sake it is also tilled, receives a blessing from God; but if it yields thorns and thistles, it is worthless and close to being cursed, and it ends up being burned. (Heb. 6:4-8)

Lest we grieve or fear too much, let's remember that this Scripture is speaking of falling away into unbelief, not merely into adultery. It is possible to restore to fulness of repentance those who fall into adultery. But the remainder of this Scripture ought to be taken fully to heart, especially about how they ". . .again crucify to themselves the Son of God, and put Him to open shame."

The writer of Hebrews returned to the subject four chapters later:

> For if we go on sinning wilfully after receiving the knowledge of the truth, there no longer remains a sacrifice for sins, but a certain terrifying expectation of judgment, and THE FURY OF A FIRE WHICH WILL CONSUME THE ADVERSARIES. Anyone who has set aside the Law of Moses dies without mercy on the testimony of two or three witnesses. How much severer punishment do you think he will deserve who has trampled under foot the Son of God, and has regarded as unclean the blood of the covenant by which he was sanctified, and has insulted the Spirit of grace? For we know Him who said, "VENGEANCE IS MINE, I WILL REPAY." And again, "THE LORD WILL JUDGE HIS PEOPLE." It is a terrifying thing to fall into the hands of the living God.   (Heb. 10:26-31)

The fact that there no longer remains a sacrifice for sins does not mean that those who fall into adultery have lost their ticket to heaven! They are still saved. What it does mean is that believers who wilfully sin will not escape His judgment. When we first received Him as Lord and Savior, His blood and cross satisfied what the law states we should reap from what we sowed before we knew Him and likewise did away with the discipline we deserved from what we did before salvation.

This Scripture says that though we who know Him will be forgiven when we wilfully sin and then repent, there no longer remains a sacrifice which would take away all the due effects of our sin! Christians who knowingly sin will have to endure the mighty hand of God's discipline, regardless of how full their repentance and how complete their forgiveness!

I am aware that this teaching so far sounds so tough and frightening that many may wonder, "Well, if I'm still going to 'get it' for my sins anyway, what good did forgiveness do?" The question is itself evidence of our defection from Scripture. The due result of all sinning is death; we deserve nothing else! "The soul who sins will die" (Ezek. 18:4 — see also Gen. 2:17 and the remainder of Ezekiel 18). Forgiveness means redemption; Jesus has died our death for us. Forgiveness means restoration to fellowship with God and mankind — and so on through a long catalogue of blessings. But forgiveness does not mean we will ever be allowed to go scot-free! It is time, and past time, for us to rediscover the toughness of God's love for us and to stop presuming on the grace of God by our flippancy about sin!

That does not mean that we should not do all that I have noted above to heal those who fall into adultery. Forgiveness not only expresses God's grace and heals our hearts, it enables us to receive discipline for the love it is, and to benefit from it as God intends.

But some may be thinking: If Christians who fall into adultery can be fully restored, what do you do with such Scriptures as:

> Or do you not know that the unrighteous shall not inherit the kingdom of God? Do not be deceived; neither fornicators, nor idolaters, nor adulterers, nor effeminate, nor homosexuals, nor thieves, nor the covetous, nor drunkards, nor revilers, nor swindlers, shall inherit the kingdom of God. (1 Cor. 6:9,10)

(Much the same lists are to be found in 1 Tim. 1:9-10, Rev. 21:8 and Rev. 22:15.)

The answer is that all of us from time to time fall into one or another of those sins. Who among us can say that he never covets or reviles? Many, after receiving Jesus as Lord and Savior, have occasionally drunk too much. If we take that Scripture without some interpretation, heaven is going to be a mighty lonely place! I suspect that St. Paul and St. John are referring to those who make their sins a habit, not trying very hard to stop.

If I attempt ice skating only once or twice, by no stretch of the imagination could my flailing arms and scrambling legs be thought of as those of a skater! Therefore I do not identify a man who falls into adultery once or twice in his life as an adulterer. He is simply a weakened Christian who has fallen into sin. If he were to continue to sin in that way, maintaining that it's okay, he could then justifiably be called an adulterer, and he would certainly not inherit the kingdom. A man or woman may fall into homosexuality. He or she can yet be delivered and set free to live a normal holy sexual life. But those who twist Scriptures to defend homosexuality as acceptable to God and as an honorable "alternate life-style" will inherit the lake of fire they deserve if they do not repent and change!

Occasional failure does not make us the habitual sinners I believe those Scriptures actually refer to. Even oft-repeated failure ought not to "label" a person. Paula and I have counseled men and women whose compulsions had driven them to adultery again and again. Some of these had been so convicted by these Scriptures they were sure they had forfeited all chance of the kingdom here or heaven hereafter! But when God delivered them through us from the root causes, they were able to stand in Christ without falling again. For them repentance was not impossible. We must guard against legalism in such cases.

It is not the frequency of sin which is the determining factor here, but the attitude of the heart. A person may fall many times, but if he does not want to fall and does not excuse his sin, the grace of God still abounds. Therefore, when we strive to restore those who have fallen into adultery, let us be fully confident we are working for, not against the Lord in accord with Scripture.

The Body of Christ must stop presuming on the grace of Christ. We must regain holy fear and respect of God and His laws. I know of no other antidote for this presumption than the repentance I call for here — and determination to set God's laws into our hearts and minds so that we will not sin against Him (Ps. 119:9-16).

The Delusion of Too Individualistic, Self-oriented Faith

The final theological trap that induces born-anew Christians to sin (that I would discuss in this book) is our modern-day, too-individualistic, self-oriented approach to the faith. We have overstressed personal salvation until we have produced a generation of self-seeking, selfish Christians who unconsciously view Jesus as a kind of Santa Claus who is supposed to get for them all the good things of life. "I'm supposed to have everything I want, so if I don't have them by righteous means, it can't be that much against God's will if I obtain them by unrighteous means!" An adulteress on a national TV program exclaimed that God couldn't be too upset that she was living as the mistress of another woman's husband. After all, He wants her to be happy, and this man's attentions were making her feel good!

While I was pondering this modern-day phenomenon and subject, preparing to write, unbeknownst to me, our son Loren was thinking about it too, and he preached an Advent sermon on the subject. With his permission, I quote excerpts from his notes as the summation of this chapter and the book:

> "Boomer-bashing" is one of my favorite sports while in the pulpit. I'm referring to the practice of prophetically confronting the lamentable state of those born in the decade or two following World War II — the "baby-boomers." I can "boomer-bash" with integrity because I was born in 1951, wore my hair long in the 1960s in the face of daunting opposition

and marched in more than one anti-war rally, chanting slogans I only vaguely understood.

As a generation, baby-boomers have distinguished themselves in only one real way: we have exalted and deified "self" to levels unprecedented in modern times. We didn't invent self-absorption. We've only expanded on what we inherited from our forebears and have infected our entire society — from the very young to the very old — with our expansions. *Self-absorption has now become the dominant philosophical underpinning for our whole culture, secular and religious.*

Consequently, our religious orientation has been excessively individualistic and self-oriented. Our approach to faith has been, "Jesus will take care of *me*," rather than, "*We* want to change the world for Christ." More to the point, it has been, "I have been personally saved," rather than, "We are a people unto the glory of God."

As a twentieth-century people steeped in individualism, we think, "Jesus came to save ME. He came to set ME free." Personal salvation is and has been the focus of our national religious thrust for many years, but it is not the dominant thrust of the Bible. Thus this century in Christian history has been dominated by evangelists preaching personal salvation, teachers telling the Body of Christ how to become personally and individually prosperous, ministers in deliverance casting out personal demons, counselors seeking to enable personal and individual fulfillment and so on. I have no real problem with any of this except when the emphasis falls in places where Scripture doesn't put it. The theme of personal salvation is certainly present in the Bible, but the dominant emphasis lies elsewhere.

While we moderns speak individualistically, the Scriptures speak otherwise:

The people who walk in darkness
Will see a great light;
Those who live in a dark land,
The light will shine on them.
Thou shalt multiply the nation,
Thou shalt increase their gladness;
They will be glad in Thy presence
As with the gladness of harvest,
As men rejoice when they divide the spoil.
For Thou shalt break the yoke of their
burden and the staff on their shoulders,
The rod of their oppressor, as at the battle
of Midian.
For every boot of the booted warrior in the
battle tumult,
And cloak rolled in blood, will be for
burning, fuel for the fire.
For a child will be born to us, a son will be
given to us;
And the government will rest on his
shoulders;
And His name will be called Wonderful
Counselor, Mighty God,
Eternal Father, Prince of Peace.
There will be no end to the increase of His
government or of peace,On the throne of
David and over his kingdom,
To establish it and to uphold it with justice
and righteousness
From then on and forevermore.
The zeal of the LORD of hosts will
accomplish this. (Isa. 9:2-7)

Note the plural references. Verse 3, "Thou
shalt multiply the nation and increase their
gladness." Verse 4, "For Thou shalt break the

yoke of their burden and the staff on their shoulders, the rod of their oppressor. . ." Verse 6, "For a child will be born to us, a son will be given to us."

Isaiah spoke of increasing the gladness of the people of God as a people while we of this generation seem to be absorbed in seeking individual happiness, often at the expense of others. Isaiah declared that God would increase the gladness of Israel as a people, a nation, together. It's their burden He'll break, one yoke oppressing a whole people. But for too many of God's modern-day people, suffering is the cue to run off alone somewhere for a private pity party as if our burden affected no one but ourselves!

One of our ministry staff commented to me that an economic crisis might be good for the Body of Christ because then the Christians would get desperate and come back to church. From years of pastoral experience I know that the opposite would happen. The fact is that too many modern-day believers attend church for selfish reasons. Therefore in the face of crisis they would go home to have a solitary pity party and would think to punish God by their absence for letting the crisis happen. Meanwhile, caught up in the same quest for self-fulfillment, unbelievers would fill up the churches. That sounds great, but wait! After the crisis, the believers would return to church, while most of those newly religious believers, no longer perceiving a need for help, would go home. [Oh, how true this is! — my comment, having also been a pastor, for twenty-one years.]

If one rejoices, all rejoice and if one suffers, all suffer (1 Cor. 12:26). Like Paul in the New Testament, Isaiah in the Old Testament spoke of a common oppression manifesting differently in each person. It is the burden of His PEOPLE that Jesus came to lift. Our individual burdens are lifted because we are part of the people whose burden is lifted.

Therefore, if Jesus breaks the yoke, He breaks it for all of us together. If we're saved, we're saved together as a people.

"The government will rest on His shoulders" (Isa. 9:6), means not that He will be a political figure and not just that He is my personal LORD. The reference is to His Lordship over the whole people of which I am a part, the church. Our society says MY LORD. The scriptural focus is on OUR LORD. US. WE.

The images of the kingdom are clearly relational. Salvation is an "us" and "we" affair, involving covenant relationship and a call to walk together in peace.

John the Baptist was conceived just a few months before Jesus was. John's father, Zacharias, received a promise from the angel of the Lord that he and his wife would have a son in their old age and that this son was to have a high calling. The definition of his task read this way:

> And he will turn back many of the sons of Israel to the Lord their God. And it is he who will go as a forerunner before Him in the spirit and power of Elijah, to TURN THE HEARTS OF THE FATHERS BACK TO THE CHILDREN, and the disobedient to the attitude of the righteous; so as to make ready a people prepared for the Lord. (Luke 1:16-17)

This was no message of purely personal salvation. The promise pointed to a restoring of oneness and togetherness. "To make ready a people prepared for the Lord." Our culture has placed the emphasis on personal salvation, but John, Jesus and the rest of the Scriptures place the emphasis on the creation of a people, saved together, laboring together, journeying together, growing together, conquering together.

Luke 2:10 reports the appearance of the angel to the shepherds to announce the birth of Jesus, "Do not be afraid; for behold, I bring you good news of a great joy which shall be for all the people."

In Matthew 1:21 the angel speaks to Joseph in a dream concerning taking Mary as his wife, "And she will bear a Son; and you shall call His name Jesus, for it is He who will save His people from their sins."

In biblical, Hebrew culture "the people" was more than just a phrase referring to more than one person. A "people" was a recognizable group, bound by common ancestry and having something of a common consciousness. Such a group was thought of as one entity even though made up of individuals as different as night and day. Israel was referred to by one name as if the nation were a single collective man, Jacob. . . A "people" was a corporate entity, a unity, with a life affecting everyone. They held both their goodnesses and their sins in common and knew that before God all of them would share in the rewards and consequences of the goodness or sin of the few or of the one. [See Joshua 7 and again 1 Cor. 12:26.]

If we're saved, we're saved together because He came to save His people from their sins. We then work out our salvation together, live it together and labor together in service.

Matthew 1:23 says they would call His name Immanuel which means God with us. Our generation would have named Him, "God with ME."

If we own and understand what the Scripture is telling us, then we must realize that personal salvation is a nearly meaningless concept unless it has some issue in oneness with the whole people of God. I'm not saved alone. I'm saved into a people. First Corinthians 12:13, "For by one Spirit we were all baptized into one body, whether Jews or Greeks, whether slaves or free, and we were all made to drink of one Spirit."

I suggest that our overemphasis on personal salvation — the attitude that Jesus will take care of me — isn't working very well. A focus on self-fulfillment leads to sin, not to holiness. The evidence is in; I see it every day. When our motivation for coming to or serving Jesus is self-fulfillment, and He apparently fails to deliver the kind of happiness we sought, we are sorely tempted to try some other way, even to the point of seeking fulfillment in sin. The result of self-absorption is always frustration and emptiness rather than satisfaction and joy.

It isn't the Law of God that keeps me moral today. It's the Holy Spirit, my love for Jesus and my oneness with the people of God. It takes all three of those elements to do it. Weakness in any one of these elements leaves us vulnerable to the ravages and temptations of the enemy. Too many of us continually repeat our sins and fall into the same ruts again and again because we lack a sense of oneness with others. we can't feel the pain we cause. We can't identify with the needs of others as if they were our own.

Why do Christians commit adultery? Because they aren't thinking or feeling in corporate terms. At some point they became individuals seeking individual, personal fulfillment without thought for others.

The quest for self-fulfillment and an

overemphasis on personal salvation cannot produce or sustain holiness. Holiness comes from the Holy Spirit in me and my love for Jesus, but it also comes from a profound sense of accountability to others with whom I am in unity in a common life. This generation has no conscience concerning the effect of the individual on the lives of others.

But realize this, that in the last days difficult times will come. For men will be lovers of self, lovers of money, boastful, arrogant, revilers, disobedient to parents, ungrateful, unholy, unloving, irreconcilable, malicious gossips, without self-control, brutal, haters of good, treacherous, reckless, conceited, lovers of pleasure rather than lovers of God. (2 Tim. 3:1-4)

And because lawlessness is increased, most people's love will grow cold. (Matt. 24:12)

I've often asserted that adultery is impossible for me. Those who quarrel with me on that point don't understand the reason for my statement or how I've been trained to function. I'm not living for self-fulfillment. I'm not living to meet my own needs. I can therefore be in oneness with my wife and feel her joys and pains as my own. Because I carry her heart in mine, as mine, I will not inflict pain or hurt upon her by any conscious act. No temptation to momentary pleasure can over-ride that oneness with her. We sin because we are thinking only of ourselves. Conscience is based on the ability to feel the pain of others and to turn away from wrongdoing for their sake. [Does Loren's testimony sound like his father's? Why? Training! From my father's father to my father to me to Loren — four generations of fidelity and instruction.]

In this latter half of the 1980s we have seen many nationally and internationally prominent leaders fall to immorality and we cried out that God was cleansing His Church. We were right, but only partially so. God was also breaking in pieces our idolization of a religious system that fostered an overemphasis on personal salvation at the expense of our consciousness of ourselves as a people. God was calling us to redemptive fellowship with one another, to be the church, "...for we are members of one another" (Eph. 4:25).

> ...but speaking the truth in love, we are to grow up in all aspects into Him, who is the head, even Christ, from whom the whole body, being fitted and held together by that which every joint supplies, according to the proper working of each individual part, causes the growth of the body for the building up of itself in love. (Eph. 4:15-16)

PERSONAL SALVATION BY ITSELF IS NOT ENOUGH. IT DOESN'T BRING US INTO THE KINGDOM OR ENABLE HOLY BEHAVIOR BECAUSE THE KINGDOM OF GOD IS RELATIONAL. I'M SAVED INTO A PEOPLE. OUR FAITH. OUR JOURNEY. OUR MISSION. OUR LORD. OUR SAVIOR.

Personal salvation runs through the New Testament like a thread, but peoplehood, unity and oneness are like a giant beam supporting every aspect of the structure. It's not just that we're saved, but what we're saved into. What are we saved for? That we should be a people and that the nations should resort to the root of Jesse (Isa. 11:10).

Jesus became one with us. God became man. The Word became flesh (John 1:14). Union. Relationship. Heaven is a festival of friends. And the Body of Christ on earth is just a rehearsal, a practice session for eternity. He came to die and to rise again to reconcile us to God and to one another, to gather us around himself in a festival of friends, a people of God together. I am convinced that in the kingdom of heaven the Lord will find the believer I had the most trouble with on earth and make him my roommate for eternity — and we'll both love it!

— R. Loren Sandford, Pastor
New Song Fellowship
P.O. Box 211337
Denver, Colorado 80221

John Loren Sandford
Founder, Elijah House, Inc.
1000 S. Richards Road
Post Falls, ID 83854

APPENDIX

A number of organizations have sprung up, offering help to the sexually addicted. The problem is that like alcoholics, the sexually addicted are often the last to admit their condition. I list the names of these organizations and where they meet in hope that readers who have struggled with sexual sins will contact these people.

It would be a relief at least to discover that you are not an addict; and a greater relief to find others who can stand with you if are.

Paula and I have not met with any of these groups, but if, as it seems, they operate on basically the same principles as A A groups, we would not hesitate to recommend that our readers give them a try.

Organizations which offer help:

1) Sex and Love Addicts Anonymous
   The Augustine Fellowship
   Fellowship-Wide Services
   P.O. Box 119
   New Town Branch, Boston, MA 02258

2) Sexaholics Anonymous
   P.O. Box 300
   Simi Valley, CA 93062

3) Sexual Compulsives Anonymous (targeted toward homosexual men)
   P.O. Box 1585
   Old Chelsea Station,
   NY, NY 10011   (212) 340-8985

4) Codependents of Sexual Addicts
   Twin Cities COSA
   P.O. Box 14537
   Minneapolis, MN 55414   (612) 537-6904

Or, Twin Cities SAA
P.O. Box 3038
Minneapolis, MN 55403   (612) 339-0217

5) S-Anon Committed Couples
S-Anon, P.O. Box 5117
Sherman Oaks, CA 91413   1-818-990-6910

6) NASAP, The National Association on Sexual Addiction Problems
NASAP of Colorado
P.O. Box 3348
Boulder, CO 80307   (303) 499-7969

Products that help overcome life's challenges...

What Elijah House has to offer...

- **Counseling**
  ... Helping people around the world.
- **Seminars**
  ... Held in many cross-denominational churches.
- **Schools**
  ... Teaching and equipping the Body of Christ.
- **Internships**
  ... Training committed Christians and clergy to be counselors.
- **Resources**
  ... Biblical truths to heal your life in books, videos and audios.

For more information, or to schedule an appointment, 208-773-1645.

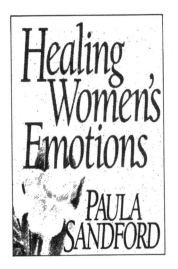

INNER HEALING CLASSIC

This sequel continues in the footsteps of **The Transformation of the Inner Man** by providing new insight and healing salve to such problems as rejection, child abuse, occult involvement and generational sin and depression.

Healing the Wounded Spirit is for everyone who suffers from hidden hurts — past or present. Through this book, God can help you to discern a wounded spirit in yourself and others and, best of all, He will show you how to receive His healing power in your life.

PROPHETIC INSIGHT

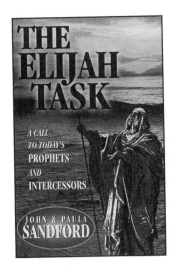

In the **Elijah Task**, John and Paula Sandford give a clear message, a balanced and practical in-depth study of the office of a prophet in the church and world today, the power and ways of intercession, and prophetic listening to God.

RESTORATION FOR THE ABUSED

With profound empathy and clear understanding, Paula Sandford ministers healing to all who have been victimized by sexual abuse — the abused child, parents, relatives and friends, as well as the abuser. She has dealt with this problem through many years of counseling and teaching, and this book shows how the victims of sexual abuse can find new life and freedom.

TRANSFORMED BY THE RENEWING OF YOUR MIND!

THE RENEWAL OF THE MIND glows with fresh insights and anointing. Its revolutionary approach will still the battleground where carnal thoughts and feelings rage. There is a solution — a process of spiritual transformation by the renewing of your mind. As you read, new peace and life will fill your innermost being.

A HANDBOOK FOR FAMILIES

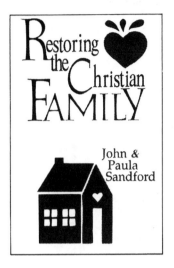

"And He shall turn the heart of the fathers to the children, and the heart of the children to their fathers" (Mal. 4:6). God is restoring families to His original purpose — to be the foundation of society, the seedbed for Christian values. Those who have discovered this treasure chest of teaching report that it has transformed their families. Fresh insights from the Sandfords' teaching and counseling ministry will enable your family to grow and develop according to God's plan.

BOOK ORDER FORM

To order additional books by John and Paula Sandford or John and Loren Sandford direct from the publisher, please use this order form. Also note that your local bookstore can order titles for you.

Book Title	Price	Quantity	Amount
The Renewal of the Mind	$ 10.99	_____	$ _____
Transformation of the Inner Man	$ 13.99	_____	$ _____
Healing the Wounded Spirit	$ 13.99	_____	$ _____
The Elijah Task	$ 10.99	_____	$ _____
Restoring the Christian Family	$ 12.99	_____	$ _____
Why Some Christians Commit Adultery	$ 10.99	_____	$ _____
Healing Victims of Sexual Abuse	$ 9.99	_____	$ _____
Healing Women's Emotions	$ 11.99	_____	$ _____

Total Book Amount $ _____

Shipping & Handling — Add $3.00 for the **first** *book,* **plus** *$0.50 for* **each** *additional book.* $ _____

TOTAL ORDER AMOUNT — *Enclose check or money order. (No cash or C.O.D.'s.)* $ _____

Make check or money order payable to: **VICTORY HOUSE, INC.**
Mail order to: **Victory House, Inc.**
                 P.O Box 700238
                 Tulsa, OK 74170

Please print your name and address **clearly:**

Name _____
Address _____
City _____
State or Province _____
Zip or Postal Code _____
Telephone Number (____) _____

Foreign orders must be submitted in U.S. dollars. Foreign orders are shipped by uninsured surface mail. We ship all orders within 48 hours of receipt of order.

MasterCard or VISA — For credit card orders you may use your MasterCard or VISA by completing the following information, or for **faster service,** call toll-free **1-800-262-2631**.

Card Name _____
Card Number _____
Expiration Date _____
Signature _____
                           (authorized signature)